NORWICH

IN THE SECOND WORLD WAR

NORWICH

IN THE SECOND WORLD WAR

NEIL R. STOREY

The
History
Press

This book is dedicated to Ray Cossey and to all who survived,
to all who helped those in need and all who lost their lives in the
City of Norwich during the Second World War.

Frontispiece: and back cover left Decontamination squad member wearing an anti-gas suit with 'Danger Gas' sign, Norwich, 1939.

Back cover middle: Photograph of Westwick Street taken by George Swain during the Baedeker Blitz on 27 April 1942.

Back cover right: *Safeguard, The Norwich Citizen's Wartime Handbook* published in May 1940.

First published 2022

The History Press
97 St George's Place, Cheltenham,
Gloucestershire, GL50 3QB
www.thehistorypress.co.uk

© Neil R. Storey, 2022

The right of Neil R. Storey to be identified as the Author
of this work has been asserted in accordance with the
Copyright, Designs and Patents Act 1988.

British Library Cataloguing in Publication Data.
A catalogue record for this book is available from the British Library.

ISBN 978 0 7509 9616 7

Typesetting and origination by The History Press
Printed and bound in Great Britain by TJ Books Limited, Padstow, Cornwall.

Trees for Life

CONTENTS

INTRODUCTION

The deep rhythmic note of the powerful engines was ominous enough and after a short period of preparation the sound was interrupted by another, the mechanical scream of heavy missiles hurtling down upon our streets and roofs, our yards and gardens. This was followed by shattering explosions, usually in series, as the 'stick' of bombs took effect. These were the high explosives of half and a quarter ton dimensions. At the same time a rain of silver fire indicated the course of the incendiaries and in a short space of time, the orange glow of great fires was visible for long distances across the quiet fields outside the city.

In the centre of the town, and far towards the outskirts, one difficulty was overcome by the very intensity of the calamity. We had been trained to move and drive vehicles with the very minimum of light … the baleful glow of flares and blazing buildings eased the hurried journey of police and Civil Defence Workers, medical and other transport … Through it all, by that sinister light, deafened by noise and blinded by clouds of smoke and dust, Norwich sped to its post of duties.

R.H. Mottram, *Assault Upon Norwich* (1945)

Norwich City firemen in action, c.1940.

So began Ralph Mottram, our city's literary doyen, in his powerful account of the infamous Baedeker Blitz air raids on Norwich in April 1942.

The city had suffered its first air raid on 9 July 1940, almost two months before a single bomb fell on London. These early raids were often conducted by a lone bomber but the damage caused to factories and homes and the resulting casualties were a sharp awakening for city residents to the nature of modern war; a new warfare where towns, cities and civilians would be subjected to aerial attack by both bombs and machine gunning conducted by aircraft based many miles away in occupied Europe.

Norwich suffered air raids in 1940 and 1941 but, having failed to destroy the Royal Air Force and failing to bring Britain to its knees with the Blitz attacks on London, major arms towns and ports, a new strategy aimed at breaking British morale by bombing the historic cities of Britain was adopted by German military strategists in 1942. Using the popular *Baedeker's Guide to Great Britain* to identify targets, a series of raids were planned on historic British provincial cities both as reprisal for damage inflicted on historic cities in Germany by the RAF and in an attempt to damage morale.

Although there were some near misses, and thanks in no small part to the prompt actions of firefighters and local fire guard parties, these raids failed to destroy the buildings that define the Norwich skyline such as the cathedral, the castle and City Hall. There was, however, extensive damage inflicted on numerous churches, historic buildings, businesses and residential areas. Hundreds lost their lives, many more were injured, and thousands had their homes destroyed or damaged. The face of Norwich was changed forever.

The most iconic and enduring images of the city during and after the air raids were captured by Norwich professional photographer George Swain; indeed, he photographed the people and events of Norwich for fifty-five years. During the air raids on Norwich and in the days afterwards, he cycled to the scenes of devastation carrying his Zeiss Super Ikonta pocket camera to record the damage and events of those dramatic times. Years later, George would reflect on those days being the most exciting period of his life but they were scary at times, too. On one occasion he even returned to find he had been so close to the fires of a blitzed area that his camera had been scorched by the intense heat.

The photographs he took of the bomb-damaged city had to be submitted to the Ministry of Information for approval before being released to the press. Swain's book, *Norwich Under Fire: A Camera Record*, first published in 1945, contained twenty-five powerful images of the blitzed city but many of his other photographs would not be seen by the general public until decades after the war.

The first book to be published on the city in wartime was by Edward Charles 'E.C.' Le Grice, who described himself as 'a spare-time photographer for the National Building Record'. Le Grice's book, *Norwich: The Ordeal of 1942*, containing his evocative photographs from areas of devastation across the city, was published shortly after the Baedeker Raids in 1942 and went into a second edition in 1943.

Swain's *Norwich Under Fire* followed in 1945, as did *Assault Upon Norwich*, which was the first official account of the air raids on the city. It contained a foreword by Regional Commissioner Will Spens and an account of the Civil Defence Organisation by Town Clerk and ARP Controller Bernard D. Storey. The main text recounting events in the city was eloquently written by Ralph Hale Mottram, who had received national acclaim for his *Spanish Farm* trilogy of novels based on his experiences as a young officer on the Western Front during the First World War.

There are also the undeservedly lesser known *The Changing Face of Norwich* by A.P. 'Phil' Cooper and Arnold Kent, and Andrew Stephenson's *Norwich Inheritance*, both published in 1948, which provided timely reminders of what was left of the old city as it embarked on its reconstruction after the war.

There were also press agency photographers and established professional and commercial photographers in the city such as Coe's, Neale and Baldry who were employed by the likes of the Ministry of Information, Ministry of Works, the police and fire service to photograph incidents and damage caused during air raids for official records. Although these photographs are often good quality and show an artistic eye, they were not originally intended for publication but they continue to come to light from a variety of sources.

There are also instances of American servicemen, particularly those involved as press and publicity officers, who had access to good cameras and film so, in addition to images of life on base and the activities of their bomb groups, there are occasional photographs of places they visited and frequented, too. An exciting discovery I made a few years back was a batch of negatives in the United States that contain high-quality animated scenes of well-known Norwich streets in 1944 that were taken by a USAAF press officer based at Horsham St Faith. These fascinating images are published for the first time in this book.

Wartime security saw restrictions imposed on the use of cameras by private individuals, and photographic film for private use was often in short supply. Small batches and occasional single images still come to light from such sources, however – George Plunkett and Clifford Temple are particularly notable for doing their best to carry on their hobbies of documenting the city in photographs as they had done before and would do for years after the war. Both of these gentlemen shared their knowledge and memories in some excellent books published in the 1980s and '90s.

In more recent years the sharing of the story and images of wartime Norwich has evolved yet again. Plunkett's son, Jonathan, has created a superb website of his father's photographs and research, and Nick Stone has created truly remarkable 'Blitz Ghost' images where he skilfully superimposes images of our bomb-damaged city streets in the Second World War over modern photographs of the locations today. Nick has also painstakingly colourised photographs of the blitzed city that add a new and engaging dimension to the images.

The documentary records of air raids on Norwich exist in a number of forms. There were official report forms and records of the fire service, police and the various wartime organisations that came under the aegis of the Air Raid Precautions (ARP) organisation (later known as Civil Defence (CD)), such as the air raid wardens, Women's Voluntary Service (WVS) and the Joint War Organisation of British Red Cross Society and Order of St John. We are fortunate that many of the original ARP/CD reports, or the duplicate copies of them, do survive and can be accessed at the Norfolk Record Office. Air raid damage reports for Civil Defence Region 4 including Norwich have also been deposited in The National Archives. The emergency services and voluntary organisations engaged in war work also compiled their own reports containing statistics and overviews of their wartime activities that have been made available to the author over his years of research and have proved invaluable in the compilation of this new volume on the city during the Second World War.

Beyond the factual reports, the human stories of wartime life, especially during the air raids on Norwich, are brought vividly to life through the personal memoirs, letters, diaries and memories of those who were actually there. When I began to research, document and record Norwich and Norfolk in the Second World War back in the 1980s there were still plenty of people around with memories and stories to tell and my appeals in local newspapers or via Radio Norfolk always received a great response. Be it trying to research a particular incident or name those who had performed a brave deed but had not been named in the press at the time due to reporting restrictions, the readers and listeners never failed to help.

Sadly, as time passes many of those who had such a remarkable fund of knowledge and memories have now passed away. I was not unique in my research and over the decades it has also been my pleasure know and count as friends many of those who were also writing books and articles or creating exhibitions and projects charting aspects of the city at war. Among them are George Swain's daughter, Judy Ball, and Joan Banger, whose superb book *Norwich at War* brought the story of the city in wartime to a new generation in 1974 and endures through reprinted and enlarged editions to this day as the key text for anyone researching the subject.

Many of the stories and photographs I collected in the 1980s and '90s were shared in my books published at that time but, as ever, after each book was published it would generate more correspondence and more new material would come to light, prompting my exclamation, 'If I only had it in time for the book!' The years rolled on and through research, purchases at collectors fairs, online auctions and kind folks still donating photographs and material to me at talks and exhibitions, more and more new material began to accumulate. Over recent years online newspapers and official documents that have been released into the public domain at both the National Archives and in local record offices provide new insights into our local wartime history.

I am particularly grateful for two major donations. First came the diaries, wartime memoirs and papers of former city librarian, the late Norman Wiltshire. In 1942 he was serving in the Royal Norfolk Regiment, based at their depot in Britannia Barracks. Among his duties at that time was librarian and drawing maps. It was in the latter capacity that Norman created a hand-drawn map of Norwich that not only shows the bomb damage across the city but names the factories, works, pubs, breweries, schools, wartime centres and other details not usually recorded on printed maps of the time. It is a unique record of the City of Norwich in wartime.

Rampant Horse Street decorated for the Silver Jubilee of King George V and Queen Mary, 1935.

I was also extremely fortunate to meet Ray Cossey at one of my talks. We clearly shared a great passion for our local wartime history and I was deeply honoured when he donated his wonderful collection of photographs and memorabilia to my care. This included a large folder of letters Ray had kept from Radio Norfolk listeners who responded to his appeal for stories for his two-part *Norfolk at War* documentary that aired on BBC Radio Norfolk in 1989. This wonderful, previously unpublished material richly deserves to be shared and, mindful that 2022 will be the eightieth anniversary of the Baedeker Blitz on Norwich, have been the driving forces for the creation of this book.

Norwich in the Second World War does not pretend to be encyclopedic but I hope it will be a useful point of reference for future generations to see what happened here and provide a timely reminder of the sacrifice of Norwich people and what they endured during the Second World War.

Neil R. Storey
Norwich
2022

1

NORWICH IN THE 1930S

In the 1939 the City of Norwich had a population of approximately 126,000 citizens, many of them housed in long rows of terraced houses that had spread out beyond the ancient walls of Norwich during the latter half of the nineteenth century. Often built more for the benefit of the property speculators than for quality, most of the properties had water on tap but many folks still had no bathrooms and their lavatory was a short walk down the back yard. Swish and modern they may not have been, and many were prone to damp, but most folks took pride in their homes and raised good, honest families. Kids played together in the back alleys and neighbours talked to each other. Like any city, there were those who suffered hard times, especially before the days of the welfare state, but communities were strong and people did help one another to get by because, who knew? It could be them needing the help and support next.

Most people who lived in the city either walked or bicycled to work and particular areas saw concentrations of people who worked in major industries local to them. Carrow had Reckitt & Colman's Mustard and Starch works, the King Street area and Pockthorpe had its breweries and public houses and along the river were timber yards like Jewson's, Read's Flour Mills and Boulton & Paul manufacturers. There were also engineering firms including Laurence Scott & Electromotors on Hardy Road and Barnard's off Salhouse Road on Mousehold. Harmer's, the clothing manufacturers, had a very fine factory on St Andrew's and many of those who lived in the terraced streets off Chapel Field Road to the south of the city were employed in Caley's Chocolate Factory.

The biggest employer in the city, by far, was the boot and shoe industry. Thousands of men and women were employed in huge factories such as Bally & Haldenstein and Sexton, Son & Everard. Some made shoes that became household names such as Howlett & White's 'Norvic' shoes and James Southall & Co.'s 'Start-Rite' shoes for children. In 1931, 10,800 Norwich people were employed in boot and shoe manufacture in twenty-six firms. By 1935,

The new Norwich City Hall and Market Place, 1938.

Advert for Norwich's famous Norvic brand shoes, 1940.

Norwich was producing 6 million pairs of shoes a year, some 16 per cent of the total British output.

The city also had three railway stations, a goods yard, a new bus station, gas, electricity and water works, laundries, joineries, coachworks and the General Post Office (GPO), which not only dealt with the post but also ran telephone lines and exchanges. In the centre of Norwich was the Cattle Market that spread across 8½ acres from the Castle Ditches, across the Cattle Market in front of the castle and around to beside Agricultural Hall Plain. In the 1930s, it was one of the largest cattle markets in the country with six firms of auctioneers and thirty-three private dealers selling 212,000 head of livestock and 100,000 head of fowl and turkey every year with an annual turnover of £1.25 million.

There was a provision market and Corn Exchange in the city centre, department stores such as Chamberlin's, Curls, Bunting's, Jarrold's and Bonds and many other smaller businesses and shops. There were also offices in the city, notably the Norwich Union Fire and Life offices that provided the city with its largest white collar employer.

The Corporation of Norwich strived hard to provide employment for those who found themselves out of work in the 1920s and '30s by undertaking numerous public works projects such as the clearance of tenements, courtyards and slums with their shared outside taps and toilets and the creation of new, good-quality council housing with front and back gardens on Angel Road and garden estates at Earlham, Mile Cross Lakenham and Mousehold that were described as 'ideal for the working man and his family – complete with electric light and bathroom at inclusive rental and rates of 9/2d per week'. By June 1938 Norwich City Council had demolished 2,280 homes, displacing 7,483 people, and had built 2,346 new homes to more than replace the lost properties. This was in the days when shops in the city would compete for business with such offers as completely furnishing four rooms in a house including pictures for the walls for £40. One enterprising store even offered to include a marriage reception for an extra £20.

There was also a rolling programme of improvement works carried out on city roads and bridges. Under the direction of the Norwich Parks Superintendent, Captain Arnold Sandys-Winsch, numerous beautifully laid out parks and gardens such as Eaton Park, Earlham Park and Waterloo Park were created for city residents to take the air, play sports, sail model yachts in the boating ponds, listen to concerts from the bandstands and enjoy themselves. These projects were well regarded and superbly executed, and in the 1920s and '30s the Prince of Wales (later the Duke of Windsor) came to Norwich on no fewer than eleven separate occasions to open public works projects.

King George VI and
Queen Elizabeth opening
Norwich City Hall, Saturday,
29 October 1938.

Norwich City Fire Brigade
demonstrating a rescue by fire
engine turntable ladder at the
Royal Hotel, on Agricultural
Hall Plain, for an Auxiliary Fire
Service recruiting event, 1939.

By the late 1930s a remarkably harmonious blend of medieval city and modern development had been achieved in and around the fine city of Norwich. Within its walls there really was a church for every week of the year and a pub for every day, not to mention a host of cafes, restaurants, tea rooms and places of entertainment such as the Theatre Royal, Maddermarket and Hippodrome for live theatrical performances. There were no fewer than sixteen cinemas, such as the Regent, Haymarket, Carlton, Odeon, Theatre de Luxe, Ritz, Thatched Theatre and the Mayfair, some of which could seat houses of over 1,000. There were also swimming baths and dance halls, every one of them with their own distinctive features, quirkiness and staff that would leave memories with those who regularly visited them for the rest of their lives.

Those who lived through the 1930s had celebrated Empire Days and Lord Mayor's Processions every year and saw the city streets decked out for King George V's Jubilee in 1935 and the Coronation of King George VI in 1937. However, when the new Norwich City Hall, the centrepiece of the redevelopment of the city centre, was opened by Their Majesties King George VI and Queen Elizabeth on 29 October 1939, it took place in front of an unprecedented number of onlookers who thronged the Market Place. Sadly, the storm clouds of war were gathering over Europe, and during the next few years the face of the city of Norwich and the lives of its people would be changed forever.

2

THE ROAD TO WAR

After the air raids suffered during the First World War, Britain was not prepared to let her air defences lapse and their reconstruction was begun in the London area in the 1920s. As the Nazis rose to power and concerns over the expansion of the German Air Force were raised, the Air Defence Intelligence System was extended to include the counties of Dorset, Norfolk and Suffolk in October 1933.

The inaugural meeting for the formation and recruitment of the Norfolk Observer Corps (OC) was held at the Norwich Lads' Club early in 1934 but the planned recruitment talk was found to be unnecessary because Norwich City Chief Constable John Henry Dain had already spoken to a number of likely local contacts and had mustered all the volunteers initially required for the new OC unit entirely from the offices of Norwich Union. By the end of November 1934, there were thirty-four OC posts across the county and a Central Operations Room under the Norwich Telephone Exchange at the corner of Dove Street and Guildhall Hill ready to communicate the path of enemy aircraft to the appropriate authorities to sound an air raid warning. The area to be known as 16 Group (Southern Area) became operational on 1 March 1935, with S.C. 'Nobby' Spalding as the first Group Controller.

In September 1935 Prime Minister Stanley Baldwin issued a circular entitled *Air Raid Precautions* (ARP) that invited local authorities to set up working committees and undertake measures such as the construction of public shelters to protect the population. Norwich City Town Clerk Bernard D. Storey, the man who would become the city's ARP Controller, recalled:

> Over the earliest preparations for defence against air attacks hangs a kind of
> unreality … During the whole of the preliminary stages, roughly from July
> 1935 to the Munich Crisis, local authorities might have been forgiven if they

had not taken too seriously the preparation of a scheme, since Whitehall itself added this saving clause to its instructions: 'These measures in no way imply a risk of war in the near future and they are wholly precautionary.'

The vulnerable situation of Norwich was recognised from early on and the City Council appointed an ARP Committee in March 1936. It held occasional meetings over the next two years, during which it devised an ARP scheme that, Storey pointed out, was 'to meet contingencies that might never arise and the nature and weight of which nobody could forecast with certainty'.

The bombing of Guernica by the German Air Force during the Spanish Civil War in April 1937 horrified the world and gave new impetus to the development of Britain's air raid precautions. Britain felt vulnerable; our mass population areas were centred on industrial areas, and predictions by British military strategists led to warnings of 'knock-out blows' being delivered to our cities within days of the outbreak of war. Estimates were that if bombing continued over sixty days as many as 600,000 people would be killed and 1.2 million injured, with mass panic ensuing.

Another estimate propounded that 100,000 tonnes of bombs would be dropped on London alone in the first fourteen days. This figure was quite an exaggeration, and exceeded the entire quantity of explosives dropped on London during the entire war, but in the years 1938 –39 the threat was taken seriously and thousands of compressed cardboard coffins for air raid casualties were supplied to City and County Council Casualty Clearing Services.

As the threat posed by Hitler and the Nazis cast its shadow over Europe, more plans were instigated to instruct the British public on what they should do in the event of a war emergency, especially the use of gas masks. Extant organisations such as the St John Ambulance, Red Cross, Boy Scouts, Girl Guides and the Women's Institute staged ARP courses and many members trained as instructors in ther own right. Early in 1938 Stella Isaacs, the Dowager Marchioness of Reading, was asked by the government to form the WVS, which was to act as a support unit for the ARP. By May 1938 its objective was:

the enrolment of women for Air Raid Precaution Services of Local Authorities, to help to bring home to every household what air attack may mean, and to make known to every household in the country what it can do to protect itself and the community.

Air Raids Precautions

A PUBLIC

MEETING

TO WHICH ALL ARE WELCOME

will be held on

Friday, April 29th, 1938

At 7 45 p.m., in

DRAYTON VILLAGE HALL

Lecturer	-	DR. MARRIOTT
Chairman		REV. WENHAM, M.A.

ADMISSION FREE

Organised by Drayton Women's Institute.

Don't Forget !   Don't Forget ! !   Don't Forget ! ! !

APRIL 29th, at 7.45 p.m.

Handbill advertising one of the first public meetings about air raid precautions, organised by Drayton Women's Institute, April 1938.

A lecture on personal protection against poison gas attack, held after hours for the staff of Green's on the Haymarket, 1939.

Norfolk was not backwards in coming forwards to start WVS branches either, and they were soon engaging in local activities.

Local businesses were keen to support their staff in ARP training and some courses were held 'in house' in city department stores and larger shops such as Curls, Bonds, Green's and Woolworths after they closed to the public. The London and North Eastern Railway converted two first-class dining cars as mobile instruction units that could also be used as cleansing stations in the event of a gas attack and these began their journey across the rail network in August 1938.

It was also in 1938 that Hitler ordered his forces to mass on the border with Sudetenland and there was major concern across Europe about what he might do next. In July 1938, the plans for Norwich Civic Week were announced and gave great prominence to ARP. A number of local newspapers ran the story:

The Norwich Air Raids Precautions Committee have approved in principle the suggestion that an elaborate A.R.P. demonstration should be held in the city during civic week in October. An intensive recruiting campaign for ARP volunteers is also under consideration tor the autumn. Some 3,500 volunteers will be needed to fill all the services in Norwich. Of this number half the posts can be filled by women. The Women's Voluntary Service organisation, which is approved by the Home Office, have offered their services in this connection. Plans are also in the course of preparation for garden air raid shelters. These will be available for any member of the public who wants them. It is estimated that the material required to construct one of the shelters, which are in trench form, would cost £3 13s. 3d.

By late September 1938 the situation in Europe had deteriorated further and Britain teetered on the brink of war with Germany. On 27 September 1938, the day before Prime Minister Neville Chamberlain flew to Munich to discuss the situation with Hitler, the trained ARP workers of Norwich were called together in Blackfriars Hall and the system of distribution of gas masks was explained to them. Teams of volunteers, many of them local women, members of the Women's Institute and WVS, worked in production lines under the supervision of trained ARP staff in church halls to assemble the supplied components into gas masks, and pack them into boxes.

The ARP workers then met at their district posts and fitted patient queues of citizens of Norwich with their gas masks. Supplies were limited and the shortfall became known to the population – some folks went so far as to catch buses to outlying towns and villages where they gave a false address to obtain a respirator. Every household received a copy of *The Protection of Your Home Against Air Raids*, which provided home owners with useful advice on

Fitting gas masks at the Norwich ARP Training Centre on Surrey Street.

protection from bomb blast and gas attack, and advised them how to select and equip a 'safe room' in their home. Public air raid shelter trenches were hastily dug in a number of areas around the city, including Chapel Field Gardens and on the Cattle Market.

The men of the 'key parties' of the various Territorial Army (TA) units in the city presented themselves at their headquarters to organise the paperwork and equipment ready for mobilisation. The Observer Corps had had its first general call out, and the emergency services had been placed on standby. An assessment had been carried out with regard to the Government Evacuation scheme whereby areas were classified according to risk of bombing. 'Evacuation Areas' were mostly London and industrial areas where children, pregnant mothers, the elderly and the vulnerable would be evacuated from. There were 'Reception Areas', initially on the coast and in the countryside believed to be 'safe from bombing', and 'Neutral Areas' where there was some risk of bombing, but children would neither be evacuated to or from these locations. Norwich and Yarmouth were classified as 'Neutral' areas, the rest of the county was designated a 'Reception Area'.

An agreement was reached with Hitler at Munich on 30 September and Chamberlain returned, holding aloft his infamous paper before the world's press, and declared he had secured 'Peace in our time'. Whether Chamberlain really believed he had achieved an accord with Hitler is still debated; what we can thank him for is that he bought Britain valuable time to prepare for war.

Auxiliary Fire Service crews with their vehicles and trailer pumps outside Norwich Fire Station, Bethel Street, 1939.

Norwich Auxiliary Fire Service crew with a fire appliance in the yard of Norwich Fire Station, Bethel Street, 1939.

One of the Eastern Counties Omnibus Company Auxiliary Fire Service crews with their fire truck and trailer pump, c.1940.

With the threat of fire bombs becoming a paramount concern, recruitment for the Auxiliary Fire Service really took off, especially after a number of high-profile displays of their work were staged around the city. Recruitment was such that the Norwich AFS could not cope with the training schedule, so Chief Officer George W. Underdown, of Carrow Works Fire Brigade, took over some of the workload and within months was training half the total number of recruits. Other businesses such as Laurence Scott, Steward and Patteson brewery and Eastern Counties Omnibus Company raised their own AFS units. Every AFS unit had the authority to requisition or hire either lorries or cars to adapt to tow trailer pumps. By 1940 there were approximately 100 Coventry Victor trailer pumps stationed in the Norwich area with approximately 100 full-time and 200 part-time auxiliary firemen to man them.

The ARP organisation had developed apace and now had a structure with a number of its own specialist 'arms', as shown in the *National Service* booklet (1939):

1. Air Raid Wardens

2. Rescue [Later further delineated to Rescue (General), and specialist Light Rescue and Heavy Rescue and Demolition Parties]

3. First Aid Parties

4. First Aid Posts

5. Ambulance Drivers and Attendants

6. Decontamination Squads [trained to remove all traces of dangerous or persistent gas dropped or sprayed from enemy aircraft from streets, vehicles and buildings]

7. Report Centres, Communications and Messenger Service

To become an air raid warden, firstly one would have to apply to Norwich City Council. The *National Service* booklet outlined the qualifications for acceptance as:

Air Raid Wardens should preferably be people who live in the district where their duties will lie. Men who are over the age of 30 are needed, and men between 25 and 30 may also apply if not available for more active service. Some women over the age of 25 are also needed.

Over the course of the war, the age stipulation for female volunteers was reduced. The rule of thumb used by many recruiters for the ARP was 'if they are fit enough and keen enough to do the job – we'll train 'em to do it'.

All air raid wardens were trained (usually on part-time courses outside of working hours) in anti-gas procedures, basic first aid and elementary fire-fighting, and instructed in how to receive, record and send messages. If passed proficient after a month of service with their unit, the new warden would be presented with their silver ARP badge. Wardens would also be given a Card of Appointment, signed by Norwich City Chief Constable John Henry Dain, to prove his or her authority to householders or others they may visit in the course of duties. In this period there were no uniforms, just a white cloth arm-band screen printed with the letters 'ARP'.

With their badge and armband came their 'appointments' of civilian duty respirator, tin helmet (painted black with a white 'W' for most wardens; white helmets with diamonds or stripes denoted the more senior ranks among the wardens and ARP officers) and an ARP-issue whistle suspended from a chain or lanyard – all of which had to be carried by a warden when on duty. Whistles and sirens were used to sound and enforce the air raid warning, and at the post

Air raid wardens for the St Benedict's Street area in 1940.

there would also be a rattle for each warden on duty to sound the warning for poison gas attack and a hand bell to sound and enforce the siren's single rising note for 'all clear' when raiders had passed.

It was the intention of the wardens Service to provide a post of five or six wardens for every 400 to 500 inhabitants. Wardens would have to acquire a thorough knowledge of their sector and inhabitants (for example, a young mother with baby twins and toddlers with husband away at the war would need assistance putting on and operating the babies' gas masks in the event of a gas attack). Wardens would also need to know the location of gas mains, electric cables, telephones, shelters and trenches. They needed to keep in touch with residents in their sector and give them necessary advice. Wardens would probably be first on the scene if air raid damage had occurred and would be responsible for summoning the proper form of help, e.g. fire service, heavy or light rescue squads, ambulance, emergency utility repair crews, etc. Such procedures were rehearsed by staging regular drills and exercises, and these operations also taught the wardens to work together and fostered strong team skills.

The problem was, from the point of view of many of the population, in the years up to the outbreak of war and indeed through the 'Phoney War' period of 1939–40 before the bombers of the Luftwaffe began their bombing campaign on Britain, wardens were sometimes viewed by their neighbours with suspicion. Dressed in just a tin helmet and armband with their civvy clothes, they did not look 'official' or 'properly appointed'.

Due to shortages in official supplies, uniforms for ARP wardens only began to arrive from October 1939. The first issue was that of a 'bluette' light denim overall for men and Macintosh-type overcoats for women with white metal buttons marked 'ARP'. Shortages persisted and many street wardens had just an armband in lieu of a uniform until 1941. Rescue workers received their overalls as a priority and some businesses donated or privately purchased blue overalls for their wardens. Navy blue battledress-style jackets and trousers began to arrive for Civil Defence workers in Norwich from 1942.

The Ministry of Home Security set up twelve Civil Defence regions across Britain, each with an appointed Regional Commissioner to co-ordinate regional officials of government departments and local authorities in Civil Defence work. Norwich was part of Region 4 (Eastern), which had its headquarters at St Regis, Montague Road, Cambridge, with Sir Will Spens as Regional Commissioner. The Norwich City Control Centre was initially established under the war memorial in the space formerly used for the storage of market stalls.

Norwich City Police special constables marching past the chief constable, senior officers and civil dignitaries on the steps of City Hall, c.1940.

By February 1939, 10,630 air raid wardens had enrolled in Norfolk, 6,000 of whom were already fully trained. In March, Norwich City Council took over one of the most modern factory sites in the city on Sussex Street to create an ARP headquarters, training school and central store, from which it established a network of eighty warden posts. The air raid wardens' appointment card was not, however, a warrant card and initially they could not enter a premises to investigate lighting infringements and would need to be accompanied by a special constable on their patrols, or it was left to beat policemen and special constables to ensure the blackout was maintained in the city.

Many policemen were ex-forces and the number of beat constables fell dramatically when the Army, Navy and Royal Air Force reserves were called up in 1939. With additional demands on the police in wartime, such as the investigation of suspicious characters – enemy 'aliens' –, the need to name enough personnel to deal with evacuation procedures in the event of invasion, petty criminals, black marketeers and the maintenance of the blackout, further recruitment was carried out to expand the numbers of the special constables and a Police War Reserve was established.

Norwich City Constabulary was one of the few to be issued with a gas van and appointed an inspector, who commenced training with volunteers from Norwich City Council. The van was equipped with a chamber that people could pass through wearing a gas mask to enable them to experience exposure to gas in an attempt to avoid panic in the event of an attack and to teach the public how important it was that the mask fitted properly and should be kept in a good state of repair.

Velma Dickie attended Hillside Avenue School, Thorpe St Andrew, and recalled their visit from the gas van:

> A small group of children went into the van with their masks on, we sat inside and talked or sang for a little while. Then a man tested the gas masks to see if the seal was tight and asked if our eyes were stinging. We then went outside and had a run around the playground, with our gas masks on. I suppose this was to clean out the mask and get the gas off our clothes.

The protection of children was paramount. They were instructed to carry their gas masks at all times and regular drills were carried out so they could practise taking cover and putting them on. Naturally, some children had been apprehensive about trying on their masks. There had been tears, but teachers did their best to encourage the children, making sure they understood their mask was important but making a game out of putting it on. Some even included a gas mask race in their sports days. Using the gas masks in their boxes like 'big conkers', was, however, positively discouraged but during the course of the war the maintenance of children's gas masks cost a small fortune.

Shelter trenches were dug in school fields and a great scheme was enacted by which many Norwich schools had underground shelters built under their playgrounds. At the end of July 1939, Norwich Education Committee authorised the expenditure of £37,000 to pay for the construction of trench shelters for its schools.

The summer of 1939 saw the emergency services of Norfolk gear up for war. Training was essential; the British Red Cross Society alone staged 289 first aid and 102 home nursing courses across the county. Smartness, efficiency and regular practise of their skills was also an important part of training for all voluntary emergency services, so training nights and parades became a weekly feature. The new recruits stood out on their public appearances in their civilian clothes and armbands as they marched with their longer-serving, fully uniformed comrades.

The first test blackout was conducted for the entire county of Norfolk between the hours of midnight on the night of 13 July until 4 a.m. on 14 July 1939. The announcement, made by Bartle Frere, Chairman of Norfolk County Council Air Raid Precautions Committee from the County Offices on Thorpe Road, was published in the local press and posters headed 'Important Notice – Air Raid Precautions' were displayed on prominent notice boards stating:

Householders and all other occupiers of premises are accordingly asked to assist by ensuring that lights in the premises are extinguished, or screened by dark curtains or dark blinds ... It is particularly desirable that external lights and other lights directly visible from the sky should be extinguished or screened by dark curtains or blinds.

It was also the first full practice for the modern air defence system, including fighter and bomber squadrons, anti-aircraft divisions, ARP organisations and the Observer Corps. Norwich ARP and emergency services staged a practice drill dealing with the effects of an imaginary air raid. Firms such as Caley's, Reckitt & Colman and Boulton & Paul suspended their night shifts in order to co-operate, while others worked through the night with minimum light. The whole scene was surveyed by Walter Riley (Chairman of the ARP Committee), the city's Chief Constable John Henry Dain and his deputy, Superintendent Herbert Balls, from a room at the top of the City Hall clock tower. They were pleased with what they saw, or rather didn't see, on that dark night with the city in pitch darkness, and they were satisfied to declare the blackout effective.

The room high in the tower above the clock proved to be an ideal position for observing the blackout. Norwich City police officers would recall they were able to view a wide area of the city and with the aid of a map they were able ascertain any district where a light was being emitted. The constable in that

Casualty handling drill for British Red Cross Society and St John Ambulance first aid parties in anti-gas suits, Norwich 1939.

area would then be called at a police phone box on his beat and would be given instructions where to locate the light. In one instance, a man on Palace Street had a small oil-fired heater in his greenhouse and even though high buildings surrounded the property, it was still sufficient to be detected. The room in the tower remained a regular air raid spotter position throughout the war.

The first batch of 300 Anderson shelters reached Norwich in late August 1939. These shelters were supplied free to all homes with an income that did not exceed £250 a year, which also had a suitable garden. Made from pre-formed corrugated sheet steel, the Anderson was supplied in twenty-one pieces with a bag of nuts, bolts and a spanner. The householder (and helpful neighbours) would join together to dig out the ground, assemble the shelter and pile a good lot of earth back on top. In Norwich the trench shelters were supplemented by sixty surface shelters. Quicker and easier to build than the underground type, these public shelters could hold up to fifty people, were constructed with 14in brickwork and were claimed to be blast and splinter proof. The first of these shelters in the city were constructed around the Cattle Market and on terraced streets where there were concreted and paved back yards rather than gardens.

The Guildhall ringed with sandbags and wooden scaffolding protection for the sixteenth-century east window.

The summer of 1939 was marked as one of bad weather, but when when the sun did shine many folks tried to have a little break away, even if it was just a day trip to the seaside. The August Bank Holiday saw LNER arrange 1,800 extra trains across their system but the visitor numbers were dramatically down on previous years. With war looming and frequent bad weather, many Londoners cancelled their holidays and the coastal resorts of Norfolk suffered badly, to the degree that local councils, hoteliers and shopkeepers from the coastal resorts sent deputations and appeals to Parliament for financial assistance.

On Friday, 25 August 1939, Hitler cut off all telecommunications beyond the borders of Germany and the invasion of Poland appeared imminent. Saturday, 26 and Sunday, 27 August was dubbed the 'silver wedding weekend' in the press because the many couples who had married during the month of the outbreak of the Great War were now celebrating twenty-five years of marriage. The rush to wed on the eve of war was no different in 1939. Many prospective couples with husbands expecting a possible call-up notice had to cancel their honeymoons, many who had been teetering on applying for their banns to be read made the decision that they would marry sooner rather than later, while others headed for the register offices.

However, Britain had now stepped up to a war footing, and for those in the military there would be no honeymoons. Over the previous days, holidays had already been cancelled for staff in banks and some of the bigger offices, and many public buildings were already belted around with sandbag walls and their window panes crossed with rubberised tape to reduce flying glass in the event of a bomb blast. It was noted that policemen were on duty with their service respirators in their issue bags slung over their shoulders and their blue shrapnel helmets stencilled 'POLICE' in white lettering carried over their gas mask bags. It was no longer a matter of if but when war would be declared.

3

CITY SOLDIERS

Being so far inland, Norwich did not provide a huge number of recruits for the Royal Navy but many a young city lad was prepared for service life from his time as a sea cadet aboard the Training Ship *Lord Nelson* on the Wensum. The major recruitment drive for RAF and RAFVR personnel to fly, crew and maintain military aircraft did not occur until 1939 and it was only in July of that year that it was announced that a RAFVR recruitment and training centre would be opening in the city. The centre was to be associated with No. 40 Elementary and Reserve Flying Training School at Norwich Aerodrome. The appeal for applications from volunteers in the local newspapers and on posters for pilots, air observers and wireless operator air gunners was very well supported by young men from across the county, notably those from public and grammar schools.

Many Norwich lads had joined the regular army, especially the battalions of Royal Norfolk Regiment, during the inter-war years at the Army Recruiting Office at 18 Thorpe Road. They responded to the offer of 'Join the Army and See the World', and most of them at least got to see India. Others who only fancied part-time soldiering could join the Territorial Army (TA). Recruits for the TA had to be between the ages of 18 and 38, but men in certain callings could serve up to the age of 50. With the consent of their parents or guardians, youths of 17 or 18 could enlist, and a few boys of 14–17 could be accepted as buglers. TA training consisted of fifteen days' camp and twenty drills a year, with twenty additional drills in the first year. Each hour's training counted as one drill. While in camp, men received pay at 2s or more a day and, if married and over 21, family allowance at 17s or more per week. In addition, trained men could draw proficiency pay of up to £5 in a year.

Those who joined the TA did so far more for the social interactions, sport and comradeship it offered. Those who became officers in the TA would recall it was very much the done thing among professionals such as solicitors, local

Officers of 4th Battalion, the Royal Norfolk Regiment at Falmer Camp, East Sussex, July 1939.

businessmen and auctioneers, with the atmosphere of the mess something akin to quite a good gentleman's club. The problem was that there had been little in the way of recruitment and the numbers who joined were nothing like there had been before the First World War.

Much to the frustration of many TA officers, despite the warning signs for months and years before, the expansion of the TA had still not been ordered, even after Munich. There were also issues with recruitment that meant that even the extant battalions were not up to strength.

Speaking at the Annual Dinner and Smoking Concert of HQ and 'A' Companies of 4th Battalion, the Royal Norfolk Regiment, held at Samson & Hercules House in December 1938, the Lord Mayor of Norwich, Mr Percy Curl, stated: 'If the voluntary system is to be maintained every facility must be given to any man who shows any inclination to join the Territorial Army'. Speaking of the apathy showed by some people in the county to join up, he thought it fair to say:

> most people considered we should not require anything but a very small army. There was a tremendous revulsion against the whole idea of war and they placed a great faith in the league of nations ... The position had changed today and we were faced with a problem greater than any we had met in the history of our country.

He concluded that he was glad employers and the Corporation were treating their employees with every consideration and was proud to announce that just 130 men were now required to bring the Norwich companies of the 4th Battalion up to strength. On 2 March 1939, it announced that the TA was to be doubled in size, and in most cases this was undertaken by 'duplicating' extant battalions, using experienced officers and NCOs to bring on the new battalions. As there was already a 5th Battalion, the 4th Battalion, the Royal Norfolk Regiment, 'duplicated' in April 1939 with a 6th Battalion, often referred to as the City of Norwich Battalion because it was raised predominantly from men in the city.

The Royal Norfolk Regiment Territorial Battalions were not the only TA units in Norwich. There were 257 and 258 Batteries of the 65th (Norfolk Yeomanry) Anti-Tank Regiment with their drill hall on the Cattle Market, which they shared with 250 Field Company and 251 Field Park Company, Royal Engineers, 243 and 244 AA Batteries, 78th Anti-Aircraft Regiment, Royal Artillery, at Ivory House and the 163rd (East Anglian) Field Ambulance on Hilary Avenue.

There were even two of the five Norfolk companies of the new Women's Auxiliary Territorial Service (later retitled Auxiliary Territorial Service) raised in the city. Women would be based at the various drill halls, with their senior commandant located in the Territorial Association building at 22 Tombland. Fortunately, a new TA drill hall was built on a 3-acre site on Aylsham Road that provided much-needed space for the new units. A huge recruiting campaign was begun, with public events in April 1939 that urged men to join as soon as possible so they would be able to attend summer camp.

The 4th Battalion, the Royal Norfolk Regiment (TA), held their summer camp at Falmer, near Brighton, East Sussex, as part of the 163 (Norfolk and Suffolk) Brigade, then still part of the 54th (East Anglian) Division in July 1939. Sadly, the lads had some of the worst wet weather of the whole summer during their time at camp. The soldiers who had been in for a few years recalled previous camps with far better weather, notably during Arundel Camp in 1937 where the beautiful setting of the Duke of Norfolk's Estate in West Sussex, the fine sunny weather and blue skies provided the men with happy memories that many would recall as 'the best of peacetime soldiering' over some very dark times that were to come in war.

'Old Sweats' would, however, reflect that the TA summer camps of all battalions during 1939 were filled with training that was more purposeful than before, and the men really felt they were gearing up for active service. Those who had recently joined up discovered that those who showed potential enjoyed the best

'Militia' recruits in training at Britannia Barracks, Norwich, 1939.

prospects for rapid promotion for a generation. Many a promising young territorial soldier came away from that camp with his first stripe and by the time of the outbreak of war some of them had even made sergeant.

Meanwhile, on 26 May, the Military Training Act 1939 (often referred to as 'The Militia Act') was passed by Parliament. It was our country's first peacetime act of conscription. The Act applied to all males aged between 20 and 21 years old and required the 35,000 men in this age bracket from across the country to answer a compulsory call-up to serve for six months' full-time military training, after which it was stated they would be transferred to the reserve for three and a half years and in that time they might be recalled in an emergency for full-time duty.

The first party of 'militia' men for the Royal Norfolk Regiment arrived at Britannia Barracks during the summer of 1939. The regular army recruits were moved into a tented camp to allow space for the militiamen to be accommodated in the barracks. By August there were 200 of these recruits at the barracks but facilities were limited. There had to be two sittings in the dining hall and there was a perpetual jigsaw puzzle to solve in fitting all the squads into the limited space available. The new gymnasium was still under construction and the number of rifle ranges really should have been doubled. It is to their credit that 'M' Company, as the militia intake were called, made excellent progress during their training. The Regimental History commented: 'the keenness shown by all concerned was a good augury for the troubles which lay so close ahead'. Most of these lads, commonly known as 'Militiamen', were still in uniform when war broke out and they were in 'for the duration'.

4

THE DAY WAR BROKE OUT

When German forces invaded Poland on 1 September 1939, Britain carried out the largest movement of people on a single day in the history of the island when it enacted the evacuation scheme. Schoolteachers in evacuation areas had been recalled from their summer holidays on 24 August and had been making the preparations ready for the 'go' signal. On 27 August notifications were received by billeting officers stating the numbers of children that would be sent to be rehomed in their area and on 31 August 1939 the order 'evacuate forthwith' was sent out by the Ministry of Health. During the course of 1 September, thousands of children passed though Norwich stations as they changed trains, or got off to catch the buses waiting for them on the forecourt to take them to safer areas in the countryside. In anticipation of the air raids expected to follow a state of war being declared, the Norfolk and Norwich Hospital cleared 284 beds for emergency use.

Army Reservists were recalled and the TA was given the order to mobilise, with all the companies of units with their headquarters in Norwich travelling into the city to be embodied. The whole operation had been long planned and went like clockwork.

The 4th Battalion, the Royal Norfolk Regiment (TA), embodied at the Chapel Field drill hall under Lieutenant Colonel John Howlett Jewson MC TD, commanding officer, and Major Alfred 'Flicker' Knights MC MM TD as his second in command. A highly respected and well liked officer throughout his long service in two world wars, Knights recorded his recollections of the mobilisation:

It was probably with mixed feelings that the order for the embodiment of the 4th Battalion, in common with all other units of the Territorial Army, was received. Memories of 1914–1918 were still in the minds of many, the War to end War had failed to achieve its object and the prospect of a further

Digging public shelters by Norwich City Hall, 1939.

Public shelters being dug on the Cattle Market, 1939.

drawn out struggle lay before us, but it was what we had been training for for years. That was the general spirit which prevailed. The early days had a spirit of excitement and thrill of impending adventure, although the actual role of the Battalion was not altogether consistent with this. Generally speaking, companies remained at their home stations viz:- Battalion HQ and HQ Company at Chapel Field Drill Hall, Norwich, A and D Companies at Great Yarmouth, B Company at Thetford, Attleborough, Wymondham and Watton, C Company at Diss, Harleston and Long Stratton.

The 6th (City of Norwich) Battalion, Royal Norfolk Regiment (TA) were mobilised at the Aylsham Road drill hall with Lieutenant Colonel D.C. Buxton in command and Major H.S. Ling MC as second in command. The old drill halls were not barracks, Britannia Barracks and the Nelson Barracks were already full and the men were needed for deployment to defend areas of the coastline and to guard places judged to be vulnerable to enemy attack, so only temporary accommodation had to be found in the city before the men were deployed.

The 65th (Norfolk Yeomanry) Anti-Tank Regiment RA had recently returned from their first camp as a newly formed anti-tank unit in Chiseldon Camp in Wiltshire. Major Alan Rees Colman, the officer commanding 257 Battery, recalled his battery concentrated on mobilisation in 1939 'in the somewhat dingy little drill hall which had served us adequately enough in Norwich from the early days of 1924 when we had started to resurrect the ashes of the Yeomanry into the semblance of a horsed 18-pounder battery'.

No. 258 Battery with Battery HQ and messing facilities set up in the sports club of Colman's Mustard Factory. Among them was Frank Potter, who joined the TA in 1939 when he was 18, preferring to choose the unit he wished to join rather than await conscription. He loved riding, so his natural choice was to join the Norfolk Yeomanry, but as he soon found out, it had been fully mechanised for some years by the time of the outbreak of war. All was not lost for Frank, however, when he discovered his battery was stationed at Norwich City Football Ground on Carrow Road and he and his pals got to realise their schoolboy dreams of having the chance to play on 'the hallowed turf' of his sporting heroes.

Having reached the age of 17½, John Curzon joined the Territorial Artillery in April 1939 and remembered mobilisation well:

On Friday 1 September at about 11.00pm there was a knock at the door and I was told to report to the All Saints Green Drill Hall, (Ivory House). With all my gear packed and saying farewell to my mother and Father, I walked from my home on Northumberland Street to All Saints Green, being stopped on the way by two policemen asking me where I was going and wishing me luck on my way. The rest of that night and all Saturday was full of tension wondering whether war would be declared.

Britain had issued Hitler with an ultimatum to withdraw from Poland or a state of war would exist between Britain and Germany and when no assurance had been received, Prime Minister Neville Chamberlain made a radio announcement to the British nation at 11 a.m. on Sunday, 3 September 1939 that Britain was now at war. Sunday services at cathedral, churches and chapels all had congregations many times their usual size and the news of the state of war existing between Britain and Germany was relayed to many by priests from their pulpits across the city.

Although tests had been carried out since March 1939, the eleven air raid sirens of Norwich sounded for the first time during the conflict just twenty-five minutes after war was announced. It was a false alarm and the all clear was given soon after. The siren wailed again at 2.45 a.m. on 4 September. Sounding as it did in the dark, waking many people from their sleep, it had a more authentic feel to it than a siren sounded in daylight. Many thought this was the moment when the bombers that had been predicted to deliver the 'knock-out blows' were coming. Wardens in the city assembled at their new, and in some cases only half-constructed and often only basically equipped, posts and the people of the city huddled in their shelters not knowing what was to come.

Mobilised members of the Norfolk Yeomanry on a route march up the Plumstead Road, September 1939.

Gunner John Curzon remembers that siren sounding as he and his comrades of the Royal Artillery slept on the floor of their drill hall on All Saints Green:

With no proper lights and everyone trying to get below in the basement, some with gas masks on, others wearing tin hats, it was almost panic stations. The all clear sounded minutes later and it all turned out to be a false alarm.

Come the morning, the people of the city had had a disturbed night but they shrugged and carried on. Gunner Curzon and his mates loaded up their trucks bright and early in the morning and moved off to Watton Aerodrome, where they were to spend the next three months under canvas preparing anti-aircraft gun sites.

Major Knights recorded the activities of the 4th Battalion, Royal Norfolk Regiment (TA), during the first weeks of the war as:

Platoon and Company Training was carried out, as far as possible, although the need for the provision of guards on vulnerable points and aerodromes made this somewhat difficult. All ranks were in excellent spirits and took both the training and the rather uninspiring tasks they had to carry out very seriously. All company localities were put in a state of defence. Gas-proof Headquarters were constructed; in fact, the company drill halls were virtually defended keeps.

The 6th Battalion was still far from up to strength so it was divided into three rifle companies with A and B Companies despatched to Hemsby, where they were billeted in the holiday camp adjoining the village. C Company took over guard duties at Watton Aerodrome and the remainder of the unit remained in billets in Norwich with HQ at the Aylsham Road drill hall as it mustered up more for its ranks.

The officers and men at the Royal Norfolk Regiment Depot at Britannia Barrack and Nelson Barracks also had a huge task on their hands dealing with the arrival of new recruits and the militiamen. As many of these lads as possible were despatched to bring the active battalions of the regiment up to strength. There were also older soldiers in the Norfolk Defence Companies, many of whom had served in the First World War, who made up the nucleus of the 8th and 9th (Home Defence) Battalions formed in November 1939.

Along with men from other territorial units in Norwich, they formed guards and a defence force around the city and its suburbs. Alan Youngman was a young soldier at Britannia Barracks at the outset of war and recalled the period well when many of the officers were veterans:

We carried on fairly normally. Gunfire at reveille (tea and biscuits) and the Officers referred to the Germans as 'The Local Bosch' or 'The Common Hun.' We made knife rests for blocking roads and filled sandbags by numbers (no kidding). We had no wireless. Signals were by LDSR or flag. Phone was through civvy operators or trunks and messages were carried by motorcycle Despatch Riders.

In the days immediately after the outbreak of war, the recruiting office in the Agricultural Hall drew hundreds of men and there were often queues out the door. Many more would have joined them but some of these men were coming from miles outside the city, leaving their jobs on farms to join up. It was still harvest time and the army made public announcements that 'they would prefer these men should not leave their agricultural work at present'.

On the streets of Norwich work gangs were out in force to complete and build more air raid wardens' posts, dig more shelter trenches and, because blackouts would now be enforced every night, paint white lines along kerbs and around lamp posts, trees and doorways at eye level. Posters were also put up to remind people to always carry their gas masks and identity cards, consider if their journey was really necessary and to take care in the blackout.

Cars, motorcycles and other motorised vehicles were also subject to blackout restrictions. The city streets were suddenly in darkness, with no street lights, no lights in shop windows and no lights casting a warm glow from people's homes. Headlamps had to be fitted with covers or masked to only allow a small sliver of light, and had to have running boards and mudguards painted white to help pedestrians and other road users spot them.

Soon, magistrates' courts would regularly have people brought before them who had been been caught out and presented with a summons to appear in court for blackout infringements. Pedestrians out at night could not carry torches unless they were very low wattage and shielded. Even someone caught striking a match to light a cigarette in the open could face prosecution.

In the immediate aftermath of the declaration of war, all theatres, cinemas and places of entertainment were closed by government order, the reason being that in the event a bombing raid the authorities wanted to avoid major concentrations of people at all costs. When the closure order was imposed there was no indication of a foreseeable reopening date. Fortunately they were permitted to open again from 15 September and managers took pains to announce in newspapers everything possible had been done to ensure the safety of patrons, all precautions had been taken to observe blackouts, all staff had been drilled in emergency duties and they were ready to act as wardens and firefighters at a moment's notice.

5

THE CITY AT WAR 1939–41

For many on the home front over the months after the declaration of war it soon seemed a very distant affair where there was no fighting, just holding the line on the French frontier. The American press dubbed the period of late 1939 into early 1940 'the Phoney War', but for those at sea in the Merchant Navy trying to get supplies through minefields and dodging U-boats or in the Royal Naval Patrol Service clearing the passages for merchant vessels and troop ships, the conflict was only too real. Imports were slashed and Britain was still trying to make up the deficit with home production, so food rationing was introduced in January 1940. Quantities of rationed food varied but a typical weekly allowance for one person would be: one fresh egg; 4oz margarine, 4oz bacon (about four rashers); 2oz butter and tea; 1oz cheese and 8oz sugar. Meat rationing followed in March 1940, weight was not specified but the weekly allocation was limited instead to any meat to the value of 1s 10d.

Many would recall that they soon got into the swing of wartime life, routinely ensuring they maintained the blackout, eating according to what was available and just carrying on. The majority of our Norwich territorials had been deployed to coastal defences in Great Yarmouth and Gorleston and around the city since late 1939 but after the Dunkirk evacuation of 1940, in which the 2nd and 7th Battalions of the Royal Norfolk Regiment suffered terrible losses, and the fall of France, the people of Britain were under no illusions: we would be under threat of invasion next.

Reports of German paratroopers being deployed in advance of the invasion forces in Holland and general disquiet among those too old to serve in the armed forces led to senior British military commanders taking the view that an armed civilian force could be raised to combat the parachute menace. As the morning papers of 14 May carried headlines of a 2,000-tank clash north of Liege, bundles of enrolment forms began to arrive at police stations and it was made known that an important announcement would be made on the BBC Home Service that evening.

A Norwich City Home Guard platoon proudly wearing their newly issued Royal Norfolk Regiment badges, August 1940.

Just after 9 p.m. on 14 May 1940, Anthony Eden, the newly appointed Secretary of State for War, made an appeal for men not in military service between the ages of 17 and 65 to come forward and offer their services in a new force to be known as the Local Defence Volunteers (LDV). The men of Norwich were not backwards in coming forward and with reams of applicants at his disposal, Lieutenant Colonel Bassett Hornor DSO, was commissioned on 17 May 1940 to raise a City of Norwich unit. Within three days, 500 men fell in at the Chapel Field drill hall. Lacking uniforms, they paraded in their civilian clothes but the Norwich lads were not to go without weaponry so they arranged to borrow some Crimean War-period rifles and were given the option of a sentry box of similar vintage from the Castle Museum. Twenty-four hours later, nightly guards and patrols were on duty across the city.

As more men decided to volunteer for military service or knew their time for call-up was quickly approaching, they were keen to get ahead of the game by learning drill and starting to get fit by attending the 'Fitness for Service Centre' (one of the first eleven to open in the country) when it opened at the football ground in June 1940. All men and boys aged 16 and upwards were welcome.

With German airfields established just across the Channel, Luftwaffe aircraft began raiding Britain – and before London had a single bomb fall on it, Norfolk was suffering 'tip and run' raids. On 9 July 1940, the city of Norwich suffered its first air raid. The day had begun fine and warm and in the newspapers over the breakfast table folks read of the Luftwaffe tactic of 'glide bombing'. The aeronautical correspondent of *The Times* wrote:

The enemy appear to be adhering, for the moment at any rate, to their policy of sending over a limited number of aircraft, splitting up some time before they reach the coast and attacking a number of points with small formations. One new feature of yesterday's raids was the employment of 'glide-bombing' in one area. To do this the bomber flies at a great height and shuts off its engines while still some miles from the objective. It then glides noiselessly over its target. The object of this method of attack is to make it difficult for the defences to locate the raider. The machine must, however, come over at a high altitude, because, with its engines off it loses height rapidly, especially when carrying a heavy bomb load. Once the bombs have been discharged the pilot switches on the engines again and regains a safer height with all possible speed.

By late afternoon cloud had extended across the sky above Norwich, providing excellent cover for any enemy raiders. The long-established Norwich engineering firm of Barnards Ltd had acquired the site of Mousehold Aerodrome on Salhouse Road for their expanding business in the 1920s and were producing armaments and miles of the wire netting they were famous for under government contracts for the military.

A few minutes before 5 p.m. a number of employees saw and heard explosions in the distance, about 2 miles away to the north. A 'Yellow' warning signal had been received but not the danger 'Red', so no siren had been sounded, indeed, shortly after 5 p.m. the 'White' safety signal had been received and staff were ready to carry on.

The noises heard by Barnard's employees had been two Dornier Do 17 bombers dropping high-explosive bombs that fell on the grounds of Sprowston Grange, damaging part of the house. Another bomb fell about a quarter of a mile away near Grange Cottage on Salhouse Road, the home of the gardener, reducing it to rubble and fatally injuring his wife, Kate Bradfield Lovett (60). She was taken to the Norfolk and Norwich Hospital, where she died the following day.

Seven or eight minutes later, the enemy bombers thundered over Barnards, flying low at approximately 600ft. Still coming to terms with what was happening, those who saw the planes recalled they were startled to see the black and white crosses on their wings and not the familiar RAF roundels. Those in the open were soon rushing for cover as a raider released a stick of bombs that fell in a straight line over the centre hangars running north-east to south-west. Most fell on open ground, sending bomb fragments, soil and grit through the air and they pierced some of the works hangars, peppered doors with holes and shattered windows. Packer Harry Dye (35) and driver Arthur Shreeve (30) were working by the loading dock when one of the bombs exploded nearby, causing fatal injuries to both men.

Despatch Foreman Ronald Green flung himself on the ground by his wood hut office about twenty paces from where one of the bombs fell. A bomb fragment tore through his right shoe, cutting the big toe, which later had to be amputated. Young Horace Middleton also lay nearby but was untouched.

Arthur Adams was standing on the steps of the despatch office at the same time. A bomb splinter went through one of his trouser legs and other splinters pierced the walls on either side of him. He felt the rush of air but by some miracle he was uninjured.

Next to be hit was No. 9 hangar, which was used for general stores. Percy Moreton, Barnard's advertising manager and warden for No. 20 office building, recorded:

The building was hit twice and almost immediately caught fire. It was soon blazing and the flames rose in a great bellying mass to a height of one hundred feet. They could be seen from many points in the surrounding district. It is fairly certain that incendiary bombs were also dropped and these – or the heat of the high explosives – ignited oil and paint which were stored respectively at the ends of the building.

The bomb that fell near the south-west doors increased the death roll. Opposite that end of the hangar stood the canteen and six workmen were leaving the building as the raid began. Two of them, Gardiner and Cullum, darted back inside, while another named Weevers ran forward and flung himself under a small bush. These men escaped injury but the remaining three caught the force of the blast. Frederick Elvin [32], trimmer and Albert Sayer [53], moulder, rushed for shelter towards the hangar doors; right into the path of the exploding bomb. Frederick Elvin was, it is believed, killed instantly and Albert Sayer died from his injuries within the hour. Sydney Cushion, a boy moulder, was badly lacerated and such was the nature of his wounds a leg had to be amputated …

The enemy raiders then divided and one of them headed towards riverside, where it dropped a stick of four bombs between the Causeway Tavern and Carrow Hill.

Two of the bombs fell on the LNER locomotive sheds and goods yard at Thorpe Station. One did not explode but the other detonated, killing Charles Freeman (44), Stanley Laffling (23), George Payne (37) and Ernest Silom (58).

Bertie Hoult (55), William Lord (50) and Richard Parker (37) were all badly wounded and removed to the Norfolk and Norwich Hospital but sadly they succumbed to their injuries. Many more were wounded to a lesser extent. Railway lines caught in the blast became a twisted and mangled mess. Many of the shattered remnants of rail were curiously left pointing skyward.

Boulton & Paul's Riverside Works suffered a direct hit on the large, aged woodworking and paint shop. This instantly caused a fire to erupt and massive columns of smoke were soon billowing skywards. The steel-framed building buckled under the heat and the truss roof and its corrugated iron covering collapsed. The sheet metal and box-making shops were also destroyed, along with the canteen, offices and boardroom. Seven died on this site, namely: Charles Bacon (36), Charles Brooks (39), Herbert Kiddell (44), Walter Smith (23), Arthur Strike (23), George Strowger (27) and Frederick Wright (16). Three men were seriously injured and removed to the Norfolk and Norwich Hospital, where John McMillan (60) died the same day, Robert Daniels (30) died the following day and Carlos Sewter (46) lost his fight for life on 12 July. Twenty more were injured.

Dick Green was a 14-year-old fire boy working as part of a team of riveters in the construction engineering department at Boulton & Paul and vividly recalled the incident when he recorded his memories of it nearly fifty years later:

> Just in front of 5 p.m. I had just refilled the tank above our fire, with crude oil, which we always did before we finished work for the day. I turned slightly to my left to step off the drum of candle oil I was standing on and was looking towards the wire netting department. To this day I can still see the blinding flash of the first bomb exploding about 40 yards away from me. The next thing I remember is holding on to the stanchion that was four or five yards to my right and the muck and the dust that had been thrown up, and above all the ringing in my ears from the explosions. When the dust had settled, down at my feet lay Mr Charlie Brooks with blood oozing from a gaping wound in his back, hardly conscious and moaning as I have never heard anybody do before.

It was knocking off time at Reckitt & Colman's Carrow Works and workers were pouring out of the gates when the raider dived and another bomb whistled down. Some of the men shouted, 'Down!' as the device tore through the trees near the old Wilderness Tower, part of the old City Wall at the top of Carrow Hill. Tragically, many girls wheeling their bicycles up the hill did not react quite so quickly and were still standing when the bomb exploded at ground level without entering the ground. Consequently, there was no cushioning effect for the blast. Bessie Upton (36) and Maud Balaam (40) were killed instantly. Several others were injured by the shrapnel, shattered glass, stones and detritus that ripped through the air. A number of the women were taken to the Norfolk and Norwich Hospital, where Gladys Sampson (18) and Bertha Playford (19), who had both been seriously injured, died shortly after admission. Maud Burrell (37) fought for her life for three days but finally succumbed to her injuries on 12 July.

In the immediate aftermath of the first raid, those directly affected by it recalled the atmosphere feeling so unreal. When confronted with such horror and one's own mortality, it is difficult for those who have never been exposed to such a thing before to get a grasp on the situation. Many would be haunted by these experiences for the rest of their lives. Dick Green wrote of how the son of the unfortunate Charlie Brooks also worked with him on the riveting team:

> We rushed off to find the First Aid man. We saw other results from the bombs as we went along the factory floor, especially one person who had been decapitated, but that didn't hold any horror to us, I often wonder why. It was too late to do anything for Mr Brooks, so all we could do was report to say we had no injuries before leaving the factory to go home.
>
> They lived on Prospect Road and I went home with him for moral support. What else can you do? I will never forget the look on his mother's face as we went up to the doorway in which she stood and told her the news. It was not long after I arrived home and felt the comfort there that I had my first cry.

One of the hard-learned lesson from the first raids was the need to provide a supplementary watch in addition to the extant public warning system. Messrs Boulton & Paul, Laurence Scott & Electromotors and Reckitt & Colman came together to pool resources and set up their own team of spotters, and a spotting post was rigged up on top of Carrow House. The firm's internal air raid signal system was then coupled up and controlled by a switch on the staging.

The spotters proved their worth over two subsequent raids but it was felt their efficiency could be greatly improved if they had an unobstructed view of the entire horizon. The joint committee worked on the problem of a more favourable location and a property on some of the highest ground in the area at No. 15 Bracondale that had been leased to Boulton & Paul was found to be ideal for the placement of a stand-alone observation post. The 'Post' took the form of a steel pylon tower surmounted by a cabin with a gallery around

The 'Crash Warning' Team who manned the 82ft-high steel pylon spotting post at No. 15 Bracondale 1940.

it from which the observers could operate – some 82ft above ground level. The spotters on the tower also proved themselves in helping to keep the factories running. In 1940 if these Norwich factories had stopped work and taken cover based on the public warning alerts there would have been 580 warnings and 640 hours and nineteen minutes taken out of the working year, whereas the spotters would only activate an alert if their factories faced imminent danger and thus just 238 'crash' warnings were given from the spotters' post with a total loss of twenty-six hours and seven minutes. Other businesses in the city, such as F.W. Harmer clothing manufacturers on St Andrew's, soon followed suit with their own spotter teams and 'crash' alert systems.

As the Battle of Britain reached its climax in September 1940, Norwich suffered more air raids. One on the night of 18–19 September saw just four bombs dropped on Norwich. Two of them were 1kg incendiaries that were swiftly dealt with, while the other two were time-sensitive SD 250kg bombs. One of these fell on heath land at Long Valley, Mousehold, and detonated twelve hours later, leaving a 30ft crater. The other 250kg bomb smashed through the path and embedded itself 20ft into the soft subsoil outside No. 4 Theatre Street. Residents were evacuated from the immediate vicinity and notices restricting entrance were posted around the area. Not deemed to be of a high priority, this bomb was left for a safety period of four days and the men from 8 Section, No. 4 Bomb Disposal Company, Royal Engineers, under Lieutenant Evlyn Jolliffe Halstead-Hanby arrived on 23 September. In 1940 there was little kit for the brave men of bomb disposal, let alone a manual to help them, so they set about digging out the bomb with their picks and shovels. It took the best part of a day's toil before the tail fin of the bomb was sighted.

Once the fuse was uncovered it soon became apparent it was a clockwork one of a new type. They knew the device could detonate and even the slightest movement could start the clockwork fuse ticking again but the working party, led by Sergeant John 'Jack' Jelley and Corporal Bertie Lawson, carried on until the fuse was suitably exposed and Lieutenant Halstead-Hanby successfully removed it.

After defusal, even when the bomb was roped around and began to be hauled up, the crew took no chances in case a secondary fuse remained hidden inside. Lieutenant Patton of the Royal Army Medical Corps carefully placed a piece of cloth on the casing and gently pressed his stethoscope on top to listen for the activation of any hidden mechanisms as the bomb was manually hauled out by block and tackle. The bomb was then loaded onto an army lorry, and Sergeant Jelley insisted that he went with it as they removed to Harford tip and the centre of Norwich was soon able to return to normality.

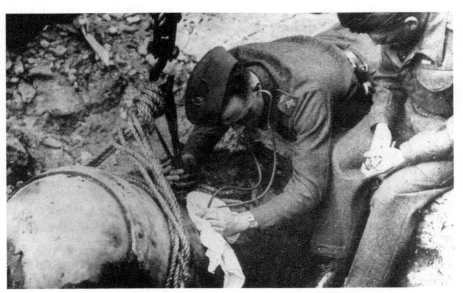

Lieutenant Patton of the Royal Army Medical Corps gently presses his stethoscope to listen for any activity in the mechanism of the Theatre Street bomb, 23 September 1940.

By a remarkable coincidence, on the day after the final removal of the Theatre Street bomb, 24 September 1940, the George Medal was introduced – and for their unparalleled act of gallantry during the blitz on Norwich, Lieutenant Halstead-Hanby, Sergeant Jelley and Corporal Lawson would all receive the medal for their roles in the disposal of the device in January 1941.

September 1940 would also be the month that the Blitz on London began and carried on, bar one night, for eleven weeks. In November 1940, twenty London firemen came to the city for a week's holiday, while a similar number of firemen from the Norwich force went down to take their place. Rather than take a holiday though, the London firemen all volunteered to serve with the city fire brigade until the Norwich lads returned.

On 2 December 1940, a single German bomber flew over Norwich when it was shrouded in fog and dropped a number of bombs across the city, damaging Wallace King's, Read's Flour Mill, Collier's and Moy's Coal Wharves and the Corona Works. Six people were killed and five injured in the raid. Two high-explosive bombs narrowly missed the cathedral. One landed in the cloister garth and exploded, throwing soil and stones as high as the tower, damaged some of the new tracery and left a 15ft crater. The other landed in the space between the Bishop's Palace and the north transept, penetrating the brick cover of a disused well and disappearing into the sandy soil below. A Royal Engineers bomb disposal team built sandbag walls around the area and began to try to

Sandbag wall and Royal Engineer Bomb Disposal crew working on the UXB that landed in the space between the Bishop's Palace and the north transept of Norwich Cathedral, December 1940.

Norwich Air Raid Wardens Division 2, Group M, Magdalen Street and Botolph Street area, c.1944.

Norwich Air Raid Wardens Division 1, Group H2, Stafford Street, c.1944.

expose the bomb so it could be defused, but as quickly as the sand was excavated from around the bomb the device just sank deeper and deeper. Eventually water was reached and the attempt was abandoned. The bomb remains there to this day.

A total of thirteen raids took place on Norwich during 1940, with a further fourteen in 1941. During 1941 a total of 661 alerts were sounded covering over 971 hours. Norwich ARP Controller Bernard D. Storey recorded:

> By no means all of them heralded a real attack; some few of them came too late unfortunately to do so. Control of the warning was not the council's responsibility, but these few unheralded incidents led high quarters to yield to the Council's urgent representations in March 1941 to authorise a public 'crash warning' system of imminent danger between the hours of 6 a.m. and 11 p.m. A locally controlled factory alarm had earlier been installed to avoid undue interruption of essential work during prolonged periods of alerts.

It was the duty of Civil Defence in the city to provide prompt help and treatment in the event of injury and to provide as well for immediate shelter, food and clothing, should need arise. At the time of the raids, each of the seventy-four wardens' posts was on the telephone to the central control room, which had direct lines to each of the five rescue party depots and four ambulance depots.

The direction of operations for all civilian services in the event of an air raid was conducted from the city's central control room under the war memorial. It was later relocated to Heigham Grove and finally (after the Baedeker Blitz of 1942) to a purpose-built building on Ipswich Road. City ARP Controller Bernard D. Storey wrote that the control room:

> would present to the unaccustomed eye an almost bewildering scene during a major raid. Messages coming in and going out on twenty-four different telephone lines; Messengers on foot taking incoming reports to the Controller, the City Engineer, the Medical Officer of Health, or their Deputies so that they might direct operations. The ARP Officer together with a Rest Centre Officer, a representative of the Wardens Service and representatives of the Post Office Telephone Service, the Gas, Electricity and Water undertakings and if necessary the Gas Identification Officer are all at hand, with liaison officers from the Police Force and the Fire Service – besides the City Architect plotting the incidents on a large-scale map of the City and the City Treasurer acting as Operations Officer. In the dark

days when invasion threatened, an Officer of the Norwich Garrison stood by to plot the movements of the enemy if he landed.

To cover the eventuality of telecommunications breaking down during raids there were fire, police and Home Guard despatch riders (on motorcycles and bicycles), and a Civil Defence messenger service was also established from a core of lads from the Boy Scouts who owned their own bicycles in the city. Their duty was to run messages between wardens in areas where communications had broken down and the report and control centre. Each of the four wardens' divisions in the city had one section of messengers attached to it and one section with report and control. Each section was then divided into four units responsible for one sector of each division under a unit leader appointed from their ranks.

Officially the messengers should have been 16 to join but one of them, Henry Hansell, would recall years later that many lads fancied the chance of a bit of adventure but, being a bit too young, they lied about their age – some were as young as 13. There was also a smaller contingent of girl messengers who were initially restricted to duties at report and control, carrying messages and internal mail between the various departments in the centre, but in time they too would do their duty carrying messages on the streets.

Ambulance drivers and crew members at their centre on Duke Street.

Red Cross and St John Ambulance units in the city recruited many more members in wartime. Enhanced by nursing auxiliaries from the Civil Nursing Reserve (CNR) and local doctors, they worked closely with the Civil Defence organisation to provide rotas of twenty-four-hour cover for their first aid posts and to train and provide crews for ambulances, mobile units and air raid relief vans. Local doctors and qualified lecturers from the St John, Red Cross and Civil Defence were also in regular demand to train and examine each new cohort of volunteers as they joined the various services in first aid and anti-gas procedures.

The Thorpe Station canteen was staffed by Red Cross and St John members between the hours of 9 p.m. and 6 a.m., when service personnel on leave would be only too grateful for a hot cup of tea and a bite to eat after long journeys. Those who worked in the canteen gave up remarkable amounts of their time when they could be sleeping or at leisure, walking 2 or 3 miles in the blackout in all weathers to take their turn on the rota. Members also helped at the St Andrew's Hall sick bay and various centres of the Blood Transfusion Service, where many were themselves donors.

On 23 July 1940, Winston Churchill, who had never liked the cumbersome and somewhat ridiculed title of Local Defence Volunteers, saw it formally announced that the organisation be renamed the Home Guard (HG). Under the national organisation, the local unit was designated 10th (City of Norwich) Battalion, Norfolk Home Guard. On 3 August the HG were affiliated to their county regiments and all Norfolk battalions were granted permission to wear the regimental cap badge and the woollen worsted battle dress of their counterparts in the Royal Norfolk Regiment. In December, the first battalion parade took place where the unit attended a cathedral service and afterwards marched past the corps commander.

As 1940 rolled into 1941 it was another cold winter and there was heavy snowfall, during which the local soldiery mucked in to help clear the roads in and around the city. As various military units got back up to strength after the losses they suffered during the Battle of France and formations were rebuilt or created anew, East Anglia saw a host of infantry, tanks and armoured forces use its countryside for manoeuvres. Many city kids would walk to the outskirts to watch the military activities and were particularly intrigued by the former commercial buses now painted in camouflage being used for troop transport.

On occasion, parts of the city would be used for urban fighting practice. Even the ancient bastion of Norwich Castle was used by some of Britain's first paratroops to practise scaling walls as part of a four-day exercise known as Operation Bulldog in June 1941.

Paratroops leaving Norwich Castle during the four-day training exercise Operation Bulldog, June 1941.

Private Norman Wiltshire was serving at the Depot of the Royal Norfolk Regiment at Britannia Barracks at the time and was put on traffic control for the exercise. He wrote an account of it in his diary:

20 June 1941:
> The alarm sounded at 2.00pm and the scheme was on. After pay parade I packed necessaries in my pack. Traffic control paraded in Field Service Marching Order with three blankets and an overcoat at 4.30pm. We marched out in the scorching sun, our section of 8 proceeding via Rosemary Road to our billets at 11 Thorpe Dene near our point at the junction of Harvey Lane.

Their duty for the next two days was to direct traffic and stop all buses, motor-cycles and pedestrians to check identity cards. They all complained of how hot it was in their equipment but there were consolations: 'I stopped many pretty girls. They were amused and interested mainly. Some thought we were doing it for fun.' The local householders kept Norman and his comrades well topped up with tea and cakes, and they were able to watch some of the progress of the exercise as military vehicles flashed by, the 'enemy' wearing helmets to distinguish them from the defenders, who were in side caps. On the evening of 21 June they heard the 'enemy' were 9 miles away and their planes flew over to 'bomb' the city. On the morning of 22 June the final attack was carried out:

> We heard the noise of artillery and saw enemy troops storming the pill-box guarding the railway bridge. Enemy tanks, armoured fighting vehicles and transport drove past, firing Bren guns and rifles at our troops. A mobile column of ours drove through the city. Enemy troops crossed the river and attacked the power station. Enemy planes were over and parachutists captured the aerodrome.

Back in 1940, a top secret deception scheme had been developed by Colonel John Turner's department at the Air Ministry. A unit with a deliberately vague title, based at Sound City Film Studios, Shepperton, they used film and theatrical prop- and set-building techniques to fabricate 'K' site dummy airfields, complete with film prop aircraft to decoy German bombers away from the real thing, and night-time 'Q' site airfields created with electrical lights and flare paths to appear like an RAF night-time landing ground. There were also 'QL' sites that operated at night using various lights to give the impression of blackout infringements of a big town or area of a city, and 'Starfish' sites kitted out with fire baskets and flame troughs to simulate areas hit by bombs.

Having begun with airfields, a 'C-series' civilian target decoy programme was rolled out in 1941 and 'Starfish' sites to decoy bombers away from Norwich were built on fields outside the villages of Bramerton and Little Plumstead in June 1941. By September 1941 they had both been upgraded to include QL decoys. Bramerton was intended to represent Thorpe Station marshalling yards, including Wensum Junction, Trowse and Trowse Swing Bridge, and the site at Plumstead to represent Boulton & Paul's Factory. Operated under instructions from No. 80 Wing, the RAF countermeasures unit, site personnel would set off electrically operated charges that would ignite dummy fires to simulate areas hit by bombs to entice other enemy aircraft to follow the hits and drop their bombs on these fields rather than the actual goods yard or factory.

The RAF personnel who crewed the sites were sworn to secrecy. Crews would be on duty for twenty-four hours, beginning and ending their shift at

8 a.m. If there was no attack, when not on shift duty the men would spend their time maintaining and 'resetting' the site ready for the following night.

Each site would have its own small bunker located about half a mile away. The design of each bunker was pretty standard, with a generator in one room to provide power for the site and an operations room on the other side of the entrance passage that had a direct telephone link with the control centre and the controls boards for the site. In the case of Bramerton, this consisted of a dial for the 'Starfish' and a control board with two circuits, one for the QL site primary and the other for residual lights, plus a 'Loco Glow' to represent the fire box of a steam engine that could be stoked up or damped down by a register. The bunker also provided a bomb-proof shelter for the crews.

The Starfish and QL sites, notably those at Bramerton and Crostwick, appear to have been highly convincing and are believed to have successfully drawn enemy bombs away from Norwich and onto the dummy sites in May, June and August 1942.

The need to smooth out issues over responsibility and compatibility of fire-fighting equipment between the AFS and the various local fire brigades across the country , which had begun working together for their first time during the blitz of 1940, brought about the complete reorganisation of local fire authorities into a National Fire Service (NFS) in 1941. In Norfolk the fire service became an entity in its own right, broke away from police control and established a new HQ at Whitegates, Hethersett. Norwich and Norfolk was now officially titled Fire Force 13.

The fire force was controlled by a commander with the assistance of a deputy. Each fire force was split into divisions under the command of a divisional officer, and then into two columns commanded by officers. Hours of duty were standardised to twelve hours on and twelve hours off (later amended to forty-eight on and twenty-four off), then finally amended to twenty-four on and twenty-four off for firemen, while ranks above section officer were more or less on a continuous duty rota.

Norwich City Fireman Frank Kett told his story in an interview with Ray Cossey in 1989:

I was called up in 1941 and had to go to Lady Lane to be interviewed by the police. We went to do different training in Bethel Street, which was right exciting. I enjoyed that, climbing up ladders and sliding down the pole one thing and another, that was really good, and from then on after six or seven weeks of that we went on exercises. During these exercises, which I found very boring, I thought that was a waste of time but that paid off later …

Bomb-damaged houses on Unthank Road after the air raid of 6 May 1941.

Repairs being carried out on houses at Earlham Green Lane that had been damaged by bomb blast and fragments during the air raid of 7 May 1941.

In March 1942 an exercise was staged in Norwich over two consecutive nights and the following day involving 1,400 firefighters, where blazes were supposed to have broken out at fifty different locations across the city in factories, laundries and business premises. A month later, they would be fighting many of those fires for real.

Troops from all over the country and from around the world had been seen on the streets of Norwich since the early war years. Among those from furthest afield were airmen from Canada, Poland, Czechoslovakia, Jamaica, Australia and New Zealand, there was even a gunner regiment from Newfoundland. However, a problem emerged that, despite being uniformed members of the Women's Land Army (WLA), they were not officially part of the military forces and were not permitted to use forces canteens.

A remedy for this situation was opened by the Norwich branch of the WVS in 1941. The Elm Hill Club for 'Women in the Services, The Land Army and Nursing Services' offered excellent meals. There was also an information bureau, supplies of chocolate and cigarettes to buy and a lounge with a radio, newspapers and magazines. The girls could even take a bath for 1s. The club superintendent was former land girl Molly Kent, who was always especially pleased to welcome members of her 'old mob'. One Sunday after members of the WLA from across the county attended a church parade at Norwich Cathedral during War Charities Week, the little club managed to feed over 100 land girls – a very welcome meal when some of them had travelled over 40 miles after doing the morning milking to attend the service!

In 1941 a Police Auxiliary Messenger Service, smartly uniformed young lads who would carry messages and run errands to assist the city police, was established. A remarkable local organisation was also set up in Norwich between July 1940 and August 1941. The Mutual Aid Good Neighbours Association (MAGNA) was raised with the intention of co-operating with the ARP and other allied organisations to provide aid and assistance for the victims of air raids, particularly those who were suffering from shock, and to alleviate the distress of those rendered homeless after a raid. Staffed along the lines of the ARP, an appeal was launched for over 2,000 volunteers to find a 'Street Mother' for every street. Her duty would be to compile a list of aged and infirm residents and organise the householders to become good neighbours, finding out who could and would be prepared to help by temporarily offering their home to those in need after an air raid. The organiser was the indefatigable Mrs Ruth Hardy, who saw MAGNA grow to over 30,000 Norwich women who offered their homes as shelter and temporary accommodation to their neighbours. Every one of them displayed a small yellow poster in their window stating, 'A good neighbour lives here'.

In the following year, the city of Norwich was going to need all the good neighbours it could get.

Civil Defence, City of Norwich MAGNA armband (Courtesy of Roger Miles)

6

THE BAEDEKER BLITZ 1942

The year 1942 began with Norwich embarking on waste paper collections for war salvage with renewed vigour. Some 110 newsagents shops acting as collection depots and a special exhibition of war materials made from paper staged in the city. Wonderful posters went up informing people of all sorts of things that could be made for military purposes from salvaged paper, such as '20 periodicals ... 1 seat for a pilot' (built-up layers of paper made seats for air crews), while others bore images such as Hitler's face painted on a dustbin accompanied by the message 'Don't let the enemy at your back door have your waste paper'.

Films such as *Salvage with a Smile* and *Raw Material is War Material* and slides advertising the scheme were shown in city cinemas and speaker vans promoted the drive through the streets. Norwich generated 25 tonnes of paper for salvage over the first week of the appeal and could proudly announce a total collection of 375 tonnes at the end of the drive. Norwich also mustered up over £1 million in War Savings during the numerous special events, parades and entertainments for Warship Week, which ran from 31 January to 7 February, and in a return gesture of gratitude, the Admiralty sanctioned the adoption of HMS *Norfolk* by the city.

For those with family members on active service, however, it was a time of uncertainty and concern. The Norfolk Yeomanry were in North Africa and their folks back in Norwich were seeing newspaper headlines reporting the fall of Benghazi in January and the British being forced back to the Gazala line.

The entire 18th Division, including the 4th, 5th and 6th Battalions, Royal Norfolk Regiment, and a number of other Norfolk territorial units, had been deployed to Singapore early in 1942 had already engaged in hard fighting 'up country' in Johore but had fallen back to the island of Singapore by early February. Security had been tight and, although their families knew they had gone abroad, they had not been informed officially where they were fighting. However, most had come to the conclusion, based on newspaper reports, that

Photograph of Westwick Street taken by George Swain during the Baedeker Blitz on Norwich on 27 April 1942. The fire was so intense it scorched his camera.

Westwick Street in the daylight of 28 April 1942 after the first night of blitz on Norwich, viewed from near the spot where George Swain took his photograph.

they had been deployed to Malaya and were filled with dread when they saw headlines announcing the surrender of Singapore on 15 February 1942.

The impression of many at home, who relied on the press to learn what was happening to their loved ones, was that the 18th Division had more or less marched off the boats into captivity and the misconception stuck. However, the fighting for Singapore had been hard and bloody and many Norfolk soldiers lost their lives in the defence of the island. After the surrender, the Japanese were not co-operative when it came to supplying the names of those they had in captivity – nor were the British government keen to release the actual numbers of those who had been captured – so it took a long while for families to be notified whether their loved ones were among the prisoners or the dead.

There was to be some small consolation in April when news reached home that the official escape party of the Royal Norfolk Regiment, a total of thirty-four officers and men under Captain Douglas Grey, had rowed out of Singapore harbour in daylight under the noses of the Japanese. They had made it to an island and were then towed in stages by native motor launches to Java.

There was also a small group of Norwich Royal Engineers including Lance Corporal Arthur 'Gillie' Potter and Sappers Neville Painter, Jack Pond – who had parents on Wroxham Road – and Aubrey Punchard, whose folks lived on Womersley Road. These lads were determined that they were not going to be taken prisoner, so at daybreak they got into a lifeboat and 'made a dash for it'. They had some rations and water with them and additional supplies of coconuts from natives. Blessed with good luck to avoid detection by the enemy and hard work taking it in turns to row for twelve days, they eventually reached Sumatra. There they found a camp to rest, recuperate and sent word home of what had happened to them.

For the majority of families there was no more news other than an official notification that their husband, father, son or brother was 'Missing in Action' and they were left in limbo for months before they heard anything more. Appeals for information from families of missing servicemen appeared regularly in local newspapers. The majority of next of kin received further official notifications in July 1942 confirming their loved one was indeed a prisoner of war in Japanese hands. Some even received the brief postcards POWs were permitted to send, but for other families there would never be a clear answer either way. Eventually the dreaded official letter would arrive stating their loved one was presumed dead and a widow's pension could then be awarded, but many never knew for certain what had happened.

Despite those at home in the city doing their best to carry on, the war was not going well, and to many minds it was now dragging on. People were becoming 'war weary' and the losses of so many local men in Singapore hit morale hard in the city. Norwich school teacher Mrs Sarah Williams was a Mass Observation diarist and summed the mood up well:

People seem to be becoming apathetic about the war. They don't argue about it, as they used to. Mr H says 'If beer disappears, we shall have lost the war' and Mr B says 'We have lost it already, so why worry?' Perhaps it's because it's the end of winter but the crusading spirit is gone, or seems to have done so.

The air raid siren had sounded, but Norwich had not experienced a raid for eight months and many people had become tired of responding to what they considered 'false alarms'. Some had taken to ignoring them and rolling over and going back to sleep if the siren sounded at night. People had even become

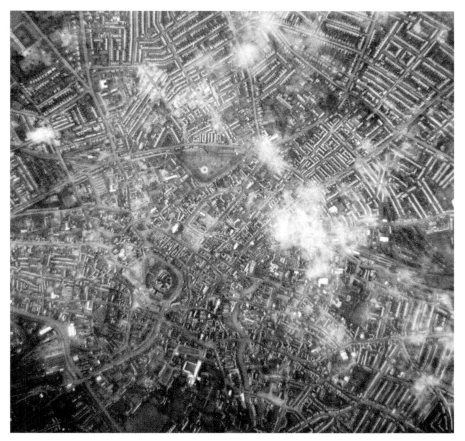

Aerial photograph of Norwich taken by a Luftwaffe aircraft, 1942. To get your bearings, see if you can discern Norwich Cathedral with its distinctive cloister, Norwich Castle atop its mound and the River Wensum.

complacent about maintaining the blackout and Chief Constable Dain had to threaten to ban entry to Norwich by motorists after dark following a number of incidents where drivers had been careless and had caused pools of light on city streets. A number of factory managers, householders and road users had also ended up being brought before the magistrates at the Guildhall for blackout infringements and stiff fines of between £1 and £2 were regularly handed down. Against this backdrop, the City of Norwich would face its darkest hours.

After the failure of the bombing campaigns to destroy airfields and London, Hitler planned to break British morale by attempting to destroy the picturesque and historic cities of England. The cities were reputedly selected from the German *Baedeker's Guide to Great Britain*. The first attack was launched against Exeter on 23 April 1942, a direct reprisal for the bombing of Lübeck. German propagandist Baron Gustav Braun von Sturm is reported to have said after the first attack of the campaign, 'We shall go out and bomb every building in Britain marked with three stars in the Baedeker Guide', and thus the so-called 'Three Star Blitz' or 'Baedeker Blitz' became the name given by the British to these infamous raids on Exeter, Bath, Norwich, York and Canterbury conducted in April to June 1942. In the immediate aftermath of the attacks British newspapers would print German news agency claims that it was a reprisal for British raids on Kiel. However, whatever the reason, on the nights of 27–28 and 29–30 April 1942 Norwich suffered its heaviest raids of the war.

The briefing notes issued to the Luftwaffe squadrons involved in the raids stated:

> NORWICH is the capital of the County of NORFOLK with 126,200 inhabitants. The city lies on the East coast of England on the hill of the Yare surrounded by many orchards. In the City besides the old Cathedral, a further 30 churches, Norman Castle, City Hall and the St Andrew's Hall. Furthermore Norwich has important rail junctions and is the central hub for several roads. There is an Aircraft parts manufacturer 'Boulton & Paul'. A bus and car factory, together with numerous other important factories.

The first priority targets in Norwich were the factory installations, while the secondary target was the inner city centre, no doubt an attempt to destroy the new City Hall.

The first indication of the incoming raiders was a radio interception as they flew over the North Sea at 2015 hours. Fighter Command scrambled night fighters to engage the raiders but no aircraft were shot down. At 23:28 on the bright moonlit night of 27 April, the first alert was sounded as two Heinkel

He 111 'X' and 'Y' Pathfinders from the 2nd Staffel of Bomber Gruppe 100 (2/KGr. 100) flew steadily over Norwich and dropped their parachute flares, which combined with the moonlight to illuminate the city streets so well that many would recall it was 'as bright as day'. The Heinkels then went into a shallow dive, dropping the first incendiary bombs and opening up with their machine guns.

Within minutes they were followed by the first wave of bombers and over the next two hours Dorniers, Heinkels and Ju 88 bombers from Luftflotte 3, comprising KG2, Gruppes I to IV, from Gilze-Rijen; Gruppe II, Gruppe III, a trainee crew from Gruppe IV and II/KG40 in Dornier 217s; KGr.506 and IV/ KG30 in Junkers 88s and Heinkel 111s from IV/KG55 and IV/KG4, dropped high-explosive bombs and incendiaries over the city and surrounding suburbs. According to the KG2 unit history, their target, marked by their 'X' beams, was the Midland & Great Northern Railway city station and it was there that the first bombs made their mark. The bombers that followed used the fires of the station as their marker.

Norman Wiltshire was a soldier at Britannia Barracks, the depot of the Royal Norfolk Regiment, during the Baedeker Raids and wrote in his memoir:

The *Eastern Evening News* for Monday 27 April 1942 carried an account on the front page of the new 'reprisal' on Bath. As dusk and the blackout shrouded Cathedral, castle and city hall citizens of Norwich might have a felt a certain unease and foreboding reading the EEN before putting the lights out and going to bed that night.

Soon the throb of aircraft engines approaching could be heard by the groups of fire watchers on their routine nightly guard. Enemy planes were overhead. Flares like fireworks hung in the sky. Now with the crackle of machine-gun fire came the whine and crumple of falling bombs. The German bombers meant business. It was a personal assault against the city. The rain of hate from the skies was directed against hospitals and homes closely packed together in the older residential parts of Norwich. The Heigham Street area suffered badly. Incendiaries set fire to many houses and high-explosive bombs destroyed others, killing or injuring indiscriminately the men, women and children who lived in them. More raiders droned overhead, finding the city by the light of the fires burning below. They met with little opposition.

A school used for a rest centre was hit, another bomb fell on the Norwich Institution for the Blind and the City Station railway yards attracted the attention of the bombers. The bombs seemed to fall in groups of three of four. Rows of small terraced houses collapsed. Those in street and garden

Norwich City Station after being turned to a fiery inferno on the night of 27–28 April 1942.

Servicemen clearing up the debris on Oak Street after the Baedeker Blitz of April 1942.

shelters heard the ring of the fire bells as the fire service went into action in the glass and rubble-strewn streets. The Air Raid Precautions and ambulances services were also in action. The short but savage attack over, the fire fighting and rescue work went on through the night.

The incendiaries that hailed down on the city started a number of large fires that were recorded as visible from a distance of 150km by the last of the Luftwaffe bomber crews. With their target so clearly marked, the Luftwaffe bombers could treat this as a 'tip and run' raid. A total of 185 high-explosive bombs fell on the city that night, killing 162 people and injuring 600. Norwich Fireman Frank Kett recalled the night well:

On the night of the blitz I was off duty, I had to report back when the siren went. Got on my bike, went to Mile Cross Lane, riding down Mile Cross Lane where the machine gun was going on I and another fireman which I met up coming along, dived into the banks until that was over. Then we carried on, got down to the station. Soon as we got down to the station and signed in I said we've got to go to Oak Street, they're in Oak Street. So we carried on from there and there was flares and incendiary bombs dropping round us.

When we got to the top of Wensum Park one of the air raid wardens come out and he said 'Oh you can't go down here there's an unexploded bomb' so we had to turn back and go towards St Augustines, and when we got there we found the school porchway was littered all over the road with a heap of rubble. So we had to manhandle this and move it all out the way so the pump could be pulled over. Then we went down to Bakers Road and pushed the pump over some waste ground in Oak Street, set the pump in, ran the hose out and running up at the side of us was Divisional Officer Collow, he said 'Come on lads' and helped us along with running the hose out.

Just as we got to the edge of the park there was a whistle right close. So we threw ourselves down onto the ground and there was a terrific explosion blowing dust and muck and rubble all over us. Anyhow, we got up, carried on with the hose and got stuck into this fire. We couldn't do much about saving it but the building next door, which was a pub, well we had to save that and sprayed water all out of the pump walls to keep that. Anyhow, when we'd finished that it was daylight and the publican, he come out, he said 'Come on lads here's a drink for you.' He had us stay stood out there and come out with two half pints of beer – cor that went down like wine. That was lovely and as we sat there two girls come up, they must have been only teenagers, just with a coat on or a mac over the top of their nightclothes, and wiped our faces with clean handkerchiefs.

The damage on that night included the city's main water pumping station, which was put out of action and meant the fire pumps that so desperately needed the water to extinguish the fires did not have the water pressure or supply to allow them to work effectively. Consequently, the railway station was turned into a fiery inferno and completely destroyed. Among the casualties was popular National Fire Service Company Officer Sam Bussey (39), who had been trying to save horses from blazing stables on nearby Oak Street when a bomb fell close by, also wounding fireman Len Strivens and Malcolm Pease. Bussey was the only full-time fireman to be killed during the Norwich blitz and was given a funeral with full honours at St Faith's Crematorium.

The raid lasted just over half an hour, during which a total of 185 high-explosive bombs weighing over 50 tonnes were dropped and hundreds of incendiaries clattered down on to roofs and streets. The rescue teams did an incredible job, working tirelessly through the raid and into the day to pull eighty-four people out alive from the rubble of their collapsed houses. As a result of the air raid a total of 162 men, women and children lost their lives and over 600 people were injured. The night had been horrific, but still the people of Norwich carried on as best they could.

Left: NFS Senior Company Officer Sam Bussey.
Right: NFS honours funeral for Sam Bussey at St Faith's, 1942. He was the only full-time fireman to be killed during the Baedeker Blitz on Norwich.

Norman Wiltshire continues in his memoir:

Next morning a tired and rather shaken city woke to survey by daylight the extent of the damage … On Wednesday evening the Lido announced dancing as usual and readers changed their books at the public library in Duke Street, where a list of casualties were posted. There was a boom in reading and dancing and in the blackout life was continuing in the way that was considered normal for the years of war.

On the night of 28 April, Norwich had a short respite when the bombers of the Luftwaffe turned their attention to the city of York. During the day of 29 April, Norman Wiltshire met his girlfriend, who was serving in the ATS, outside the Odeon cinema on Botolph Street:

We walked along bombed streets – St Augustines, Angel Road, Philadelphia Lane, passing by roads blocked by debris and unexploded bombs and eventually reached the Capitol [Capitol Cinema, Aylsham Road]. We walked on to the Falcon Hotel and went, had two brown ales and then drank a gin and lime to a quiet night.

Edge of the crater on Barn Road caused by the bomb that blew up the ruins of St Benedict's Gates, 30 April 1942.

Both then returned to their barracks, but sadly their hope for a quiet night would be dashed shortly after the siren was sounded at 21:13 on 29 April 1942. Before the dust and smoke of the fires of the first raid had ceased, forty Luftwaffe bombers were over Norwich, dropping their first bombs on the city at 23:25. This attack was led by seven Heinkel He 111 Pathfinders from Chartres. The main bomber force that followed comprised seventeen Dornier Do 217s of II/KG2 from Soesterberg and eleven from III/KG2 at Schiphol. A further eight Do 217s of I and IV flew from Gilze-Rijen. Nine crews came from IV/KG55 and a further nine from II/KG40 from Soesterberg. Five came from IV/KG4 and fifteen Ju 88s were drawn from IV Gruppen of KG3, KG30 and KG77, all operating from Chievres.

Norman Wiltshire was on fire-watching duty that night at Britannia Barracks and had a panoramic view of the city from Mousehold during the attack:

Sirens warned of the return of enemy aircraft for a second 'reprisal' raid on Norwich. Flares again lit up the sky as the raiders flew low over the city dropping incendiaries. Fires were started, salvoes of high-explosive bombs crashed into burning buildings and Norwich was again under attack but this time there were more signs of battle. Fairly heavy anti-aircraft fire was directed against the attackers as they dived low over the streets of the city.

The Crown public house (right) on St Benedict's Street looking toward Dereham Road after the air raid of 29–30 April 1942.

Safeguard, The Norwich Citizens War-time Handbook, published in May 1940.

Bertie Cossey's certificates for attendance at anti-gas training and incendiary bomb control courses, 1940. A typical pair of qualifications for a Norwich air raid warden.

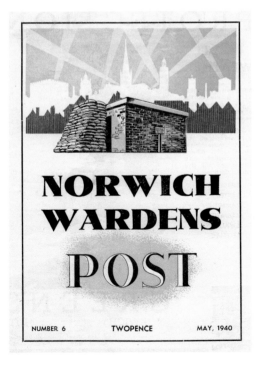

Norwich Wardens Post, the in-house journal for Civil Defence services in the city, May 1940.

You wouldn't refuse a cup of tea to a wounded soldier or an Air-raid victim

— then you won't refuse to

GIVE YOUR PENNIES EVERY WEEK

to the Norfolk War Charities when the Collector calls

What is a penny ? . . . the cost of a cup of tea . . . the price of a cigarette.

In other counties the Red Cross is asking for a penny. Here in Norfolk we are asking for more than that. Why ? *As well as the Red Cross and St John,* we have 23 other charities relying on us.

We depend on your pennies — and 24 charities, including the Red Cross Penny-a-Week Fund, depend on us.

Norfolk alone in the country raises money in the name of *all* war charity. Prove that Norfolk's way is the best way.

> You live in a house . . . . . the bombed are homeless.
> You have warmth . . . . . . our seamen face the winter gales
> You are in England . . . . . but what of the prisoners of war ?
> You have so much they haven't—and we ask so little.
> Just your pennies . . . *every week.*

Please let Everyone in your home read this.

Wartime leaflet appealing for donations for Norfolk war charities.

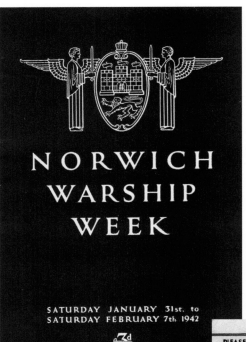

Cover of the programme of events for Norwich Warship Week, 31 January to 7 February 1942.

NORWICH WARSHIP WEEK

SATURDAY JANUARY 31st. to SATURDAY FEBRUARY 7th 1942

PRICE 3d

Air raid precautions local information card issued to households in the Elizabeth Fry Road area of Norwich, January 1941.

PLEASE HANG IN CONVENIENT PLACE FOR QUICK REFERENCE

CITY OF NORWICH

AIR RAID PRECAUTIONS
IMPORTANT TO EVERY HOUSEHOLDER

1. This card is issued on behalf of the A.R.P. Committee of the City Council. It should be carefully studied and kept and the information brought to the notice of all members of your household.

2. **KNOW YOUR WARDENS.** Your nearest Warden's Post is

   Elizabeth Fry Road by Lubbock Close

   and is the link between you and the vital services. It is most important that you should afford every help to the Wardens attached to the Post. If possible get to know them now and ask if there is anything that you can do to help. They may be glad for you to have a bucket of sand or water standing in your garden in readiness for an emergency. If so let them know exactly where the bucket is and keep it filled. In the event of any unexploded bombs or other missiles dropping on or near your premises, the occurrence should be reported as soon as possible to the patrolling Wardens or to the Warden's Post or to a Police Officer.

3. **LIGHTS. Be very careful of your lights whether from windows or opened doors, skylights or torches.** If you go out to a shelter, be sure to turn off the lights in your house before you leave. Turn off your gas at the main if there is a raid on the City.

4. **GAS MASKS.** If you want advice about your gas mask, go to your Warden's Post, but if you wish to exchange or replace it, apply to one of the undermentioned Warden's Divisional Headquarters:—

   1, Rackham Road.   3, Milverton Road.   11, West Parade.

5. **PROTECTION AGAINST GAS ATTACKS.** Carry your gas mask always. If you have been in contact with Gas and your **clothes** are contaminated go home quickly or go to a friend's house, discard your clothing before going indoors, have a bath and put on clean clothing.

   If your eyes are affected by gas, or if you have inhaled gas or if any part of your body is affected by gas spray or vapour, go to one of the First Aid Posts mentioned in paragraph 6. The best way to protect yourself from gas is to stay in your shelter (if you have one) or remain indoors. If the shelter or room is not gas proof, wear your gas mask. Everybody who has no other duties to perform should adopt these precautions when gas has been used. The wardens will endeavour to warn you of the presence of gas by using their rattles.

6. **CASUALTIES.** If you have received injuries but can walk, go to one of the under-mentioned **First Aid Posts** :—
   Norfolk and Norwich Hospital
   Colman Road School
   Sussex Street A.R.P. Headquarters (Entrance Baker's Road)
   Thorpe Hamlet School, St. Leonard's Road

7. **INCENDIARY BOMBS.** Keep a look-out for these on your house or your neighbour's. Deal with them promptly either with a stirrup pump or with sand or soil. If you have none of these things at hand, call the Wardens or the nearest voluntary Fire Party or a neighbour who has a stirrup pump or other means of putting a fire out. Everyone, ordinary householders as well as owners of business premises, must learn one of the great lessons of the war. Their first protection against fire is not the brigade, it is themselves. Only by the united work of ordinary men and women, not by fire services alone, can we be saved from the enemy's worst weapon. **Fires are beacons which tell following enemy planes where to drop their H.E. Bombs.**

P.T.O.

Watercolour painting of the first night of the Baedeker Blitz on Norwich, 27 April 1942, as seen and painted by Corporal W.C. Buck, 1942.

The following maps showing where bombs fell on the City of Norwich were hand drawn by Royal Norfolk Regiment soldier and later city librarian Norman Wiltshire after the Baedeker Raids of April 1942. High Explosive bombs are denoted by a dot and and radiating lines, incendiary bombs by crosses and areas of extensive fire damage caused by incendiaries and HE explosions are shaded grey. The area on the map below shows the city centre from King Street and the Castle to Chapelfield Road.

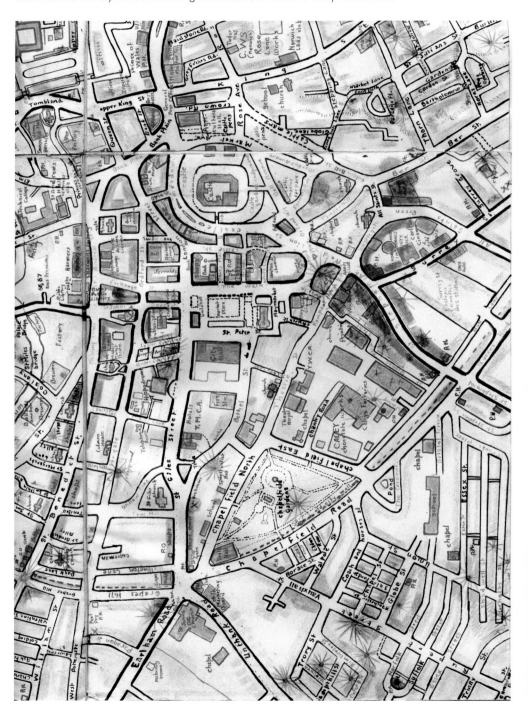

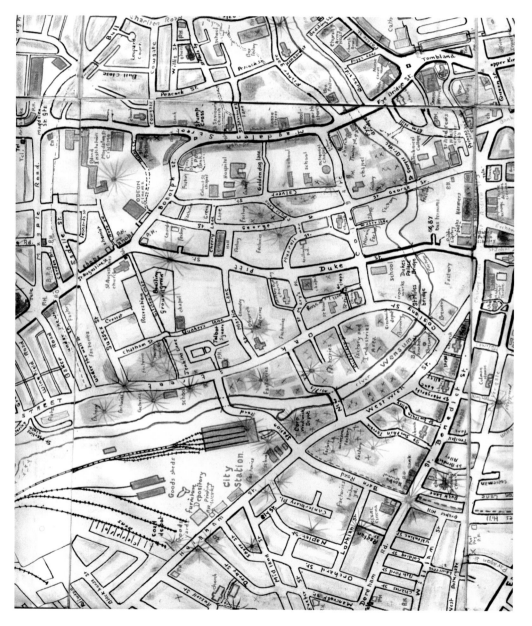

Bomb damage map showing the St Benedict's Street, City Station, Heigham Street and Magdalen Street area.

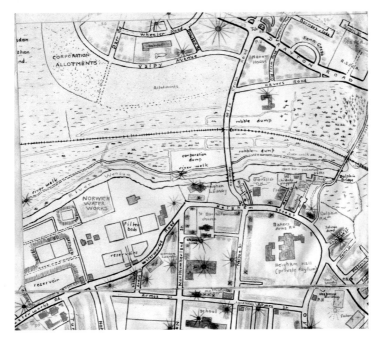

Bomb damage map showing North Heigham, Norwich Waterworks and Mile Cross area.

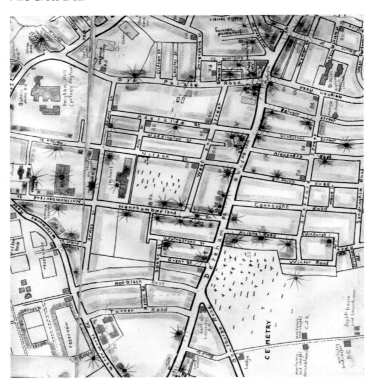

Bomb damage map showing the Dereham Road area.

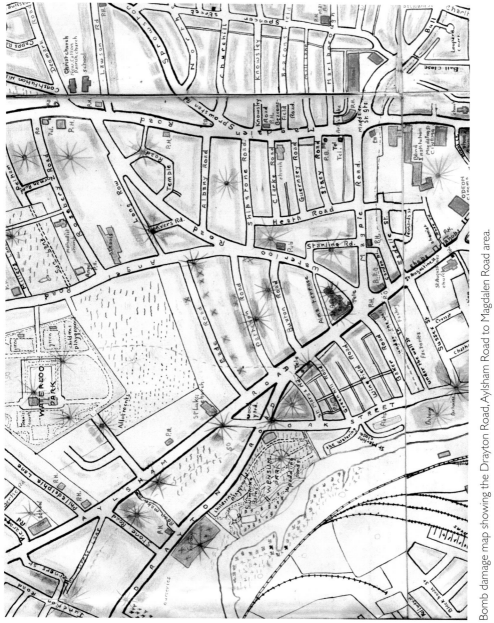

Bomb damage map showing the Drayton Road, Aylsham Road to Magdalen Road area.

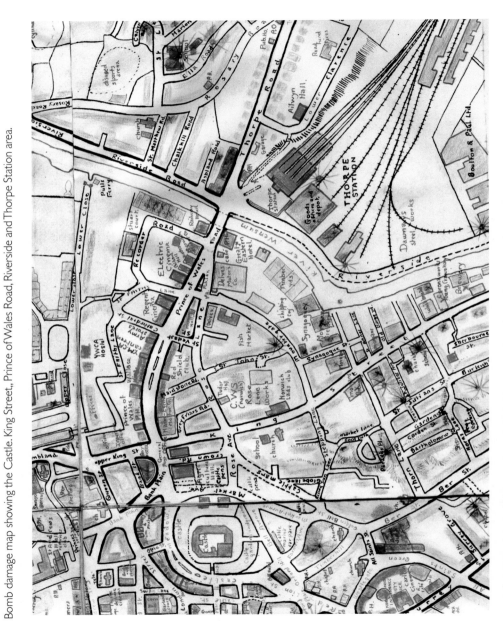

Bomb damage map showing the Castle. King Street, Prince of Wales Road, Riverside and Thorpe Station area.

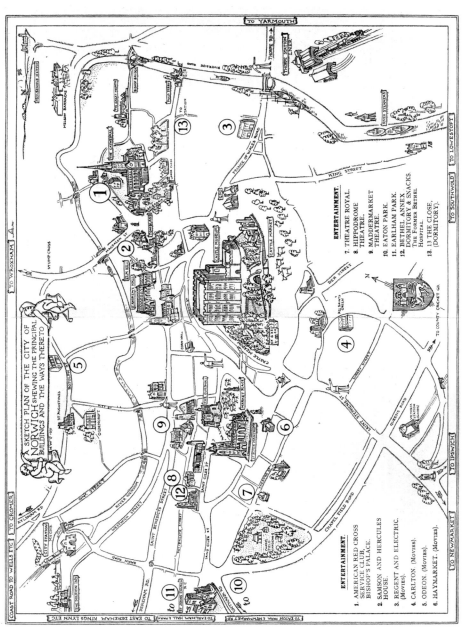

Sketch plan of the City of Norwich showing principal historic buildings and places of entertainment produced for US service personnel by the American Red Cross Service Club, 1943.

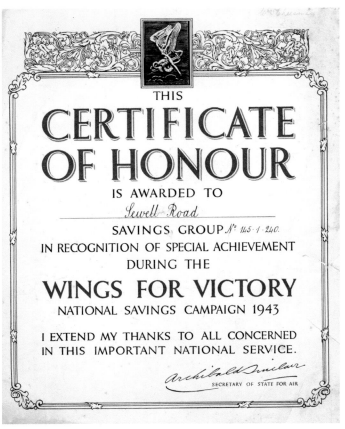

THIS

CERTIFICATE OF HONOUR

IS AWARDED TO

Sewell Road

SAVINGS GROUP Nᵒ 145·1·240.

IN RECOGNITION OF SPECIAL ACHIEVEMENT

DURING THE

WINGS FOR VICTORY

NATIONAL SAVINGS CAMPAIGN 1943

I EXTEND MY THANKS TO ALL CONCERNED
IN THIS IMPORTANT NATIONAL SERVICE.

Archibald Sinclair

SECRETARY OF STATE FOR AIR

Certificate of Honour presented to the Sewell Road Savings Group in recognition of their special achievement during the Norwich 'Wings for Victory' savings campaign, 1943.

NORWICH

SALUTES THE SOLDIER

through

THE ROYAL NORFOLK REGIMENT

SOUVENIR PROGRAMME 1944

NORWICH "SALUTE THE SOLDIER" WEEK JUNE 10-17

Cover of the programme for the Norwich 'Salute the Soldier' week, 10–17 June 1944.

Mrs. Sleigh.

CITY OF NORWICH

Final Parade & March Past of the Norwich City Home Guard

SUNDAY, 3rd DECEMBER, 1944
At 10.45 a.m.

ADMIT BEARER

to Balcony of City Hall (entrance by "Marriage" Door opposite The Guildhall)

The Bearer must be in position by 10.30 a.m.

BERNARD D. STOREY,
Town Clerk.

Admission ticket for the balcony of the City Hall to watch the final parade and march past of the Norwich City Home Guard, 3 December 1944.

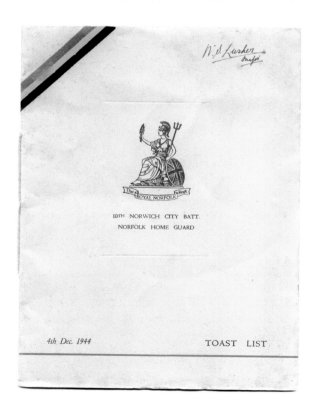

10TH NORWICH CITY BATT.
NORFOLK HOME GUARD

4th Dec. 1944

TOAST LIST

Souvenir of 10th (Norwich City) Battalion, Norfolk Home Guard Officer's stand down social evening at the drill hall, Chapel Field Road, on 4 December 1944.

"Well Done" . . .

Now that the time has come for us to 'Stand Down', may I say how very proud I am to have had the 10th Battalion under my command, and how much I have enjoyed meeting and working with all of you: I value the friendships I have made. Now you can stand down with every right to feel that you have done your duty and contributed very materially to the victory which we all of us hope may not be long delayed.

The best of luck to all of you.

Well done indeed the '10th' — may its spirit never die!

— Lt.-Col.

December 1944.

A note of appreciation from Lieutenant Colonel Bessett-Horner on the stand down of 10th (Norwich City) Battalion, Norfolk Home Guard, December 1944.

CITY AND COUNTY OF NORWICH

CIVIL DEFENCE

The Air Raid Precautions Committee of the City of Norwich express their thanks and appreciation to ____ Mr. J. Read, ____

____ 54, Stafford Street, Norwich. ____

of the ____ Wardens' ____ Service

upon the completion of an arduous period of duty ·as an enrolled member of the Norwich Civil Defence Organisation during the World War.

(Signed)

Chairman

Date ____ 2.5.45.

Certificate of thanks and appreciation from the Norwich City ARP Committee to James Henry Read for his service as an air raid warden during the Second World War.

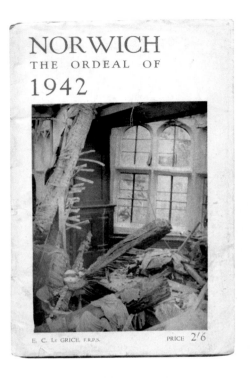

The three classic wartime accounts of the blitz on Norwich. *Norwich the Ordeal of 1942* by E.C. Le Grice FRPS (1942); *Norwich Under Fire* by George Swain (1945); *Assault Upon Norwich* by R.H. Mottram (1945).

The medieval St Benedict's Church and Alley after the air raid of 29–30 April 1942.

The raid lasted about an hour and a quarter, during which 112 high-explosive bombs were dropped, along with thousands of incendiaries. Local photographer George Swain documented the raid in photographs and recalled incendiaries in *Norwich Under Fire*:

> They dropped in thousands. Some went through the roofs of houses to start fires inside; others glanced off the roofs to burn themselves out in streets and gardens, or rolled down the tiles and burned in the troughs until the troughs melted. In some districts, mostly containing the homes of working people, there was hardly a street without one fire or more. Fire Guards tackled them with stirrup pumps, sand and water buckets, and so saved hundreds of houses but whole rows were burnt out.

Norman Wiltshire also recorded what he saw:

> The chandelier flares in the sky were not needed now by the bombers, widely scattered fires cast a fearful glow for miles around as Norwich appeared to be alight from end to end. Having dropped their bombs the raiders, harried by night fighters of the RAF, turned for home. The NFS men fought the fires

Damage to a street shelter and many houses on Essex Street after the air raid of 29–30 April 1942.

The ruins of Caley's Chocolate Factory on Chapel Field after the air raid of 29–30 April 1942.

through the night, the dead and injured were cared for and the homeless con-
fused and bewildered found shelter for the remainder of the night. A smell of
dust, rubble, smoke and gunfire pervaded streets cluttered with broken glass,
bricks and snaking fire hoses.

In this raid, about half of the 90 tonnes of bombs that were dropped met their
mark. Far more incendiaries were used, severe damage was sustained and was
made more severe because the Heigham Street water works had been disabled
in the previous raid, causing major problems for the fire service. A total of
sixty-nine people lost their lives, 198 people were injured, eighty-nine of them
seriously. The main target this time was the city centre with Thorpe Station
and Goods Yard, Bishop Bridge Gas Works, the Water Tower and Boulton &
Paul's works as the secondary targets. The city centre and City Hall remained
remarkably undamaged, the nearest bomb landing on the Clover Leaf Cafe
on Guildhall Hill. The Hippodrome was also hit, blowing two house managers down the stage door steps, incredibly, without hurting them. The blast
ripped the back out of photographer George Swain's adjoining studio (narrowly missing George, who was on the premises at the time) but killed Harry
Pitchford, the stage manager, his wife Gertie and performers Anders and
Dagmar Pederson.

The area across the Market Place, Brigg Street, St Stephens and Rampant Horse
Street were the scene of dreadful devastation as firebombs gutted building after
building, including Curls and Bunting's department stores, Woolworths and
the centuries-old thatched Boar's Head pub on the corner of Surrey Street.
On Chapel Field Road, Caley's Chocolate Factory was also burnt out. Many
local children risked life and limb over the ensuing days to get among the
rubble and into the lower stories of the building, where the vats of chocolate
had ended up releasing their precious contents. Despite being riddled with dust
and bits of masonry, children grabbed chunks of chocolate, which had been
rationed, and gorged themselves, many of them eating so much they were sick.

The area of the city from St Benedict's Street, up along Dereham Road and
across North Heigham was badly hit in both raids. The area around and including the historic St Benedict's Gates (the St Benedict's side of what is now the
Grapes Hill traffic lights) was reduced to rubble and a huge crater was left by
a high-explosive bomb. The nearby Wincarnis works off Westwick Street was
left a burnt-out shell and large sections of Grapes Hill and Barn Road were
also devastated. St Benedict's Church was reduced to little more than a wall
and a bomb-scarred tower. To give an idea of the level of destruction here,
among the rubble there appeared to be a pillbox that no one could recall being

St Stephen's Street after the air raid of 29–30 April 1942. The burnt-out shell of the Boar's Head on the corner of Surrey Street is in the background.

Looking across the ruins of Curls department store on Rampant Horse Street towards Orford Hill after the air raid of 29–30 April 1942.

there before. Then it clicked, it was the strong room and all that was left standing of the Midland Bank!

Edward Le Grice, the author of *Norwich, The Ordeal of 1942*, recalled:

> The outstanding remembrance is of the choking dust and smell of soot and gas, for the blast certainly acted as a chimney sweeper par excellence. On the night of April 29th, our family sheltered under the stairs – I had been told by an expert that a cupboard under a strong staircase offered the best possible protection – and so it proved in our case, and in many others … Bomb after bomb fell shaking the house to its foundations, for we counted 29 HE [high-explosive] bombs within a few hundred yards of us. Windows were shattered, ceilings crashed down, the crockery on the cupboard shelves was shaken off, a sugar basin emptied itself on my daughter's head, to be followed by the milk jug and finally when one bomb fell just opposite, the voice of a Warden was heard to say 'Don't you think you had better come out of there?'

Olive Wright was living on Old Palace Road, off Dereham Road, at the time of the raid:

> I was in the air raid shelter with the rest of my family. It was very uncomfortable, as we had to lie stretched out across the floor, head to one side, feet to the other, with no room to bend our knees, as we were all too tall. But this discomfort faded that night as we heard the planes dive-bombing and saw the reflection of flames through the opening of the shelter, and heard the crackling of burning buildings around us. I felt like an animal caught in the middle of a bonfire. I was shaking uncontrollably, and praying, as I think we all do in times of extreme terror. When the air raid was over, my sister and I walked up Old Palace Road and saw where a pub had taken a direct hit, so we joined in a line of people who were passing pails of water to douse the fire.
>
> Our house was hit and destroyed that night by a land mine that landed on the road outside. There was nothing left of our home except for one wall, standing tall, on which there was a hook and my best dress fluttering like a flag … Eventually we all went down to St Barnabas Parish Hall, where a team of ladies were giving out food and drinks. We stayed there for about three days. My mother, who had been nearest to the opening of the shelter, suffered bomb blast to her legs, and was unable to walk. She had trouble with her legs for the rest of her life.

ARP Controller Bernard D. Storey remembered first light after the raid:

> There was no doubt that the Germans had set out to destroy the city and it
> looked as if they were succeeding. A high wind helped them but in spite of that
> the street guards and NFS kept the fires in check. It was hot work while it lasted
> and it lasted long after the all clear had sounded and the first streaks of dawn
> appeared. I remember what a lovely dawn it was, calm and mild, with the sun
> shining pink through the smoke and people with smoke-stained faces walking
> in ruined streets, glad to be alive but saddened by the destruction of homes and
> shops that had been familiar from childhood. How still the air seemed!

Many people who recall those dreadful nights freely confess they not only
thought that when the daylight came there would be no city left – indeed, some
thought the end of the world had come. Whole streets, businesses, churches and
pubs were destroyed, burnt out or damaged beyond repair.

The symbolic historic buildings of Norwich such as the cathedral, castle,
Guildhall and City Hall, however, were all still standing after the raid. Some
would even suggest that Hitler had given specific orders for the bombers to
avoid the City Hall because it had the longest balcony of any civic building
in Europe and the Führer wanted it for him and his cronies to stand on as the
victorious invasion forces of Nazi Germany goose-stepped by.

AFTERMATH

Norfolk had suffered air raids and casualties since 1940 but the Baedeker Raids
on Norwich of 27–28 April and 29–30 April 1942 were unprecedented in the
sheer scale of destruction across the city. A number of volunteer members of wartime emergency services, wardens, Home Guard and fire watchers were killed or
injured while doing their duty, and on some streets three or four members of a
single family lost their lives. Everyone seemed to know someone who had been
hurt. Norwich would never experience such loss of life through bombing again.

One death through bombing is one too many but, considering the scale
and intensity of the attacks of April 1942, the loss of 231 lives could have
been a lot worse. The problem was that the casualty figures were not released
immediately after the raids; it was impossible to do so because the search of
the bomb-damaged urban areas had only just begun and there were still many
people displaced and missing. A rumour of hundreds of deaths became magni-
fied in each retelling to thousands killed in the raids as it spread across Norfolk

and East Anglia. In an attempt to crush this dangerous rumour, Will Spens, the Regional Commissioner, issued the following statement, which was reproduced in all local newspapers and quoted in many of the nationals:

Last week there was a large number of rumours in the Region. Many of these had no foundation in fact. What was alleged to have taken place or to have been said had not taken place or been said. Where there was foundation, the facts were grossly exaggerated. To take specific cases; Heavy attacks were alleged to have taken place on towns which were not attacked at all. Broadcasts were alleged to have been given which were not given. The number of persons killed at Norwich was in some cases multiplied tenfold by rumour. I appeal to all persons in the Eastern Region to set an example by disbelieving rumours, by not passing these on, and by being pretty short with those who do. They can in that way be of real service to the country.

One story that has been repeated to the author again and again, which lingers beyond all others in the 'popular memory' of the bombing of Norwich, is the Chapel Field Gardens shelter 'disaster'. The story tells of an underground shelter in the park that received a direct hit and so many were killed and could not be recognised that authorities just decided to cover it over and leave the bodies down there. After considerable research and independent interviews with a number of the rescue party members who attended the scene, it can be categorically stated that no such major disaster actually occurred and no bodies were left buried within the shelter.

The root of the story, like all the best urban legends, has some truth in it. An underground public air raid shelter on Chapel Field Gardens did receive a direct hit on the first night of the bombing of the city on 27–28 April 1942. In fact, four 500kg bombs fell on Chapel Field Gardens that night, two hit the shelter but one did not explode. Rescue parties were quickly on the scene, getting people out of the wreckage and treating the injured regardless of the unexploded bomb (UXB). Everybody else was kept at a distance by police and air raid wardens until the bomb was defused at 0700 on 28 April. It did, however, give passers-by plenty of opportunities to see stretcher after stretcher being carried out to nearby waiting ambulances. The story of the Chapel Field 'disaster' had enough of a ring of truth about it to stick ever since.

One of those who went public with his account of what actually happened at the shelter was rescue worker 'Ozzy' Osbiston who, in a newspaper article in 1977, pointed out that there were actually only three fatalities, which he recalled as 'Two sisters named King and a soldier named Warren.' The roll of civilian war dead held by Commonwealth War Graves confirms these as sisters Honor and Doris King, aged 14 and 16 respectively, who had lived with their family not far away from the shelter on Chapel Field Road. The third body was the dead soldier who had been mentioned in the local press as directing people into the shelter at the start of the raid but he was not named. Thanks to Osbiston's recollections and the CWGC Debt of Honour Register, he can now be identified as 33-year-old Private Frederick Thomas Warren, Royal Army Ordnance Corps. His body was returned for burial near his family and home and he rests in Islington Cemetery, Middlesex.

The burials of over 100 victims of the Norwich air raids of late April 1942 were conducted in a special avenue of Norwich City Cemetery at Earlham over 4, 5 and 7 May. Today each grave is marked by a metal plaque along the kerb that stretches along what is now a green, gated, garden-like avenue. Originally each grave was marked with a white cross bearing the name and age of the air raid victim painted in black lettering on the cross bar. Some graves contained more than one family member and their grave markers were annotated accordingly. Flowers were planted in a long row at the foot of the graves and there was room for family memorial vases for floral tributes.

The number of people who had been rendered homeless as a result of the two nights of bombing ran into the thousands. For some, misfortune had followed tragedy after salvaging clothes and effects from their shattered houses after the first raid and putting them into storage in the city, only for them to be destroyed in the next attack. However, the relief efforts provided by the voluntary wartime organisations was truly magnificent.

From half an hour after the sirens sounded, mobile canteens manned by members of voluntary services were on the scene, serving tea, cakes and cigarettes to firemen, the recued and rescuers. Salvation Army canteens distributed hundreds of cups of tea and biscuits. Six YMCA vans worked in relays to keep a constant flow of refreshment and their crews continued to report for duty even when the bombs were falling. The twenty Church Army vans in the city served 10,000 cups of tea during the raids and thousands of meals were served by the eleven rest centres established by the education authority and welfare organisations. Bernard D. Storey commented on the work of the rest centres:

> No one can speak too highly of the work done by the Rest Centre Staffs. The 13 first-line centres in the city's day schools offered shelter, food and drink to numbers often in excess of 2,000. In reserve were nine more fully equipped centres and another 24 that offered emergency refuge.

A Salvation Army clothing distribution centre was opened on Cow Hill, along with another rest centre at Lakenham. The WVS also distributed a large amount of emergency clothing, held in storage ready for distribution to those who had been bombed out. Fifteen cases of clothing were also sent to Norwich to help replace clothes lost during the bombing by friends of the British Legion in America. The WVS also supervised the removal of furniture from bombed houses and provided hundreds of staff for rest centres in the city. MAGNA was also to the fore, and many members had sheltered people in their own homes, 400 temporary homes were found for the homeless and valuable assistance, advice and first aid was rendered to people across the city.

A tribute to the duties performed by Boy Scouts during the Baedeker Blitz on Norwich was published in both local and national newspapers:

> Nearly 400 Scouts were on duty during and following the recent ferocious 'reprisal raids' on Norwich. Their fearless service in spite of fires, dive bombing and gunfire, has won the admiration of all who came in contact with them. They carried messages without thought of personal safety and fought incendiaries until every available sandbag was used and carried out cheerfully and efficiently all the jobs allocated to them.
>
> The Scouts' after blitz service proved a most valuable organisation. For hours on end the boys worked tirelessly in their distribution of notices, in guiding people to rest centres, getting them onto evacuation buses, re-uniting them with families, getting information for inquiries from soldiers, sailors etc about their relatives, helping emergency food vans and centres, shifting furniture by trek cart and lorry, cooking for the stranded people in empty houses and by fields and commons, helping feeding arrangements for incoming police, firemen and rescue men from outlying districts and guiding these to required points and a hundred and one things, not forgetting the Animals' First Aid Post which dealt with hundreds of injured cats and dogs.

The Norwich Scouts headquarters at Lower Close had been damaged in a previous raid but the Scouts had tidied up and made five of the twelve rooms habitable for the use of bombed-out people. The raid of 27–28 April, however, saw the complete destruction of the building and all equipment and personal kit was lost. But still they carried on.

There was even an ENSA company of entertainers who had played their popular 'Crackers' review many times before. The raids did not deter them and they gave performances through the raids and then went to help ARP and rescue workers after the show. Their fortitude received the thanks of the Chief Warden.

The author's grandmother, Kay Storey, was a St John Ambulance volunteer at North Walsham. She had seen the glow of the fires of Norwich in the sky and knew it would not be long before the call would come for her to report to the ambulance depot. With well-liked local sweet shop owner Tom Payne as driver and Kay as attendant, when many would be thankful they were safe and miles away from the burning city, they headed out as fast as they could, ambulance bell ringing through the blackout along the Norwich Road.

As they approached the built-up areas of the city, they saw streets strewn with the broken glass and rubble from destroyed and damaged homes, and as the fire crews fought the flames rescue crews were pulling people out of the rubble. For some victims there was nothing that could be done. The doctors present would check for vital signs but if they just shook their head the rescue crews had to press on in the hope of rescuing the living. Those they could help were given the first aid they needed and Tom and Kay made run after run to the hospital and back, through streets where the windows of houses belched fire and streamed up the walls.

Kay remembered vividly how the corridors of the hospitals were soon filled with raid victims and how the dust clung to their hair, their clothes often torn and black with the soot and smut of the fire and collapsed chimneys. Some had faces streaked with tears running through the grime on their faces, but they were glad to be alive. Memories of that night stayed with Kay for the rest of her life and brought tears to her eyes if she thought too long about them. She was not unique; Kay and Tom were just two of hundreds who came to the aid of the stricken city.

Assistance came from far and wide. There were rescue parties, ambulances and fire crews that came from across the county and as far away as Letchworth, Watford and St Albans in Hertfordshire, Bedford and Luton in Bedfordshire, and Brentwood, Chelmsford, Colchester and Southend in Essex. A mobile unit consisting of three travelling vans and marquees was also sent up from the City of London. Staffed by helpers who had honed their skills and experience during the London Blitz, they established a relief depot at the Model Senior Girl's School on Dereham Road to provide shelter, replacement clothing and personal items to those who had been 'bombed out'.

The British Army and Royal Air Force also provided parties to help with the rescue efforts, ambulances to transport the injured and manpower for the clearing of bomb-damaged areas. The men of the Scottish Horse, at that time a medium regiment of the Royal Artillery, had been based nearby and did so much in these efforts that they were presented with a silver cup by the city in recognition of their work during the bombing.

There were numerous acts of gallantry by both uniformed services and civilians during those nights of the blitz. Many would go unrecognised but meant so much, sometimes even life and death, to those they helped. Among the first to be honoured for their courage during the Baedeker Blitz on Norwich were Inspector Charles Buttle of Norwich City Police, Air Raid Warden Charles William Shore, Fire Guard Staff Officer Franklyn William Horsley and Senior Company Officer James William Waller (Norwich) NFS, who all received British Empire Medals. Divisional Officer William Collow, No. 13 Fire Force Area (Norwich) NFS, was presented with an MBE. The citation for his award states:

> During enemy air attacks on Norwich Divisional Officer Collow contin-uously led his officers and men and at all times displayed cool, calculated courage and magnificent determination. He led the various units right up to the actual points where they were detailed to operate and set a courage example under direct hazards of exploding bombs.

There was also an MBE for Norwich City Police Deputy Chief Constable Herbert William Balls. His citation states:

> During enemy raids on Norwich Mr Balls set an outstanding example of courage and devotion to duty. He attended major incidents in the danger zones to direct operations and displayed initiative and leadership without regard to his own safety.

The young men of the Civil Defence Messenger service did sterling work throughout the blitz on the city and the story of one of their number lingers in in the memories of Norwich people. John Grix became one of our nation's youngest recipients of the British Empire Medal but he had never courted fame or recognition. He had lied about his age to join the Messenger Service; boys had to be 16 but John was still just 15 when the sirens wailed on the nights of the blitz. Joan Banger relates his story in *Norwich at War*:

> He cycled two miles to duty through the heaviest bombed area, repeatedly jumping from his machine to lay flat as bombs whistled down, and, when passing one building that was blazing furiously, his hands were sprayed with

acid shooting from its windows into the street. On arrival at his centre he reported for duty and throughout the night he obeyed instructions which included travelling through devastated parts of the City to lead firemen from the County to the various reported incidents.

The Messengers, unlike the other Civil Defence Services, did their work singly. Not until hours later did this boy mention that first aid was necessary for his acid-burnt hands, and afterwards, when daylight came, he volunteered to join parties of rescue workers. That night he slept at the Report Centre and the following day helped wherever he could in the city. When the siren again sounded he once more made many nightmare journeys, during which he was blown from his machine five times.

When Grix's award was announced, a *Daily Mirror* reporter went to interview him and the poor lad was rather thrown by the attention he was receiving, worried he would have to leave the Messenger Service because the truth had been exposed by the award of the medal, he commented:

I was so keen I put a year on my age, of course I never dreamed I should be caught out like this. If I have to leave the Service just because of a medal it will scarcely be worth it ... I haven't any idea what the award is for. I was just doing my duty.

HM King George VI speaking with Civil Defence Messenger Service hero, 15-year-old John Grix BEM on his visit to the city, 13 October 1942.

After those two nights of horror, it is often forgotten that the German bombers returned again in the early hours of 1 May 1942. It was probably a diversionary raid for the main raid that was aimed at Sunderland, Newcastle, Gateshead and other towns along the Tyne in the north-east of England but an estimated 700 explosive incendiaries landed across Norwich from Heigham Street to Duke Street, Harmer's clothing factory on St Andrew's Street, up along Exchange Street and caught Garlands on London Street. Seven people were injured, and one of them later died from his injuries.

In the wake of these attacks, the defences of Norwich were enhanced with the deployment of more barrage balloons, extra anti-aircraft guns and coverage by night fighter aircraft. Some would argue that the arrival of these defences, although very welcome, was in typical local understatement, 'a bit late'.

However, many people of Norwich did not realise at the time that an attack had been ordered on Norwich for the night of 8–9 May 1942. Some seventy-six aircraft of Luftflotte 3, loaded with 110 tonnes of high-explosive bombs, parachute mines and seventy-six canisters of incendiaries, took off on the mission; but thanks to the new defences and the RAF night fighters, very few of the raiders reached the city and they had to content themselves with ditching their bombs over other locations, mostly over fields around the Poringland and Stoke Holy Cross area. Only two high-explosive bombs fell on Norwich that night, both landing on the boiler house of Woodlands Hospital (now the West Norwich Hospital). The hospital was badly damaged but thankfully nobody was killed or injured.

On 26 May, the Duke of Kent paid a visit to Norwich, during which he toured bomb-damaged areas and met survivors and members of various Civil Defence organisations who had done so much during the city's darkest hours. The sirens may have wailed on a number of subsequent occasions but no bombs fell on Norwich until the night of 26–27 June 1942, when the Luftwaffe returned with a vengeance.

Heinkel He 111 Pathfinders and Junkers Ju 88s of KGr.506 and Dornier Do 217s from I, II and III/KG2 would be involved and all available aircraft, some sixty in number, were despatched for the raid. Their tactics were to circle over a wide area before the attack, many of them showing navigation lights in an attempt to confuse the anti-aircraft defences around the city. The night was still and clear, the moon shone bright in the sky and it was perfect weather for the raid. The raiders approached the bomb run shortly after 0200 on 28 June, the sirens wailed their warning and the enemy bombers were soon discharging flares that illuminated the target in eerie daylight. The raiders flew over the balloon barrage at 8,000ft and carried out a concentrated drop of 29 tonnes of high-explosive bombs and an estimated 15,000 to 20,000 incendiary bombs during a raid that lasted little more than thirty minutes.

Private Norman Wiltshire was at Britannia Barracks and wrote of the night:

> Friday 26th June as cathedral, castle and city hall were outlined against the night sky sirens warned of yet another attack on the City. Mousehold Heath was a viewpoint for the battle. Flares revealed landmarks in their familiar daytime shapes to the questing bombers in the black sky above. Norwich seemed naked, waiting to be ravaged by an unseen enemy.

About 2,500 homes, shops, businesses, schools, churches and public buildings were damaged to a greater or lesser extent in the raid. High-explosive bombs fell near Britannia Barracks and Bouton & Paul's Riverside Works, Laurence Scott and Electromotors, Victoria Station and the Thorpe Station Goods Yard, destroying a goods shed and a number of loaded trucks. Carrow Works suffered extensive damage across its site and even the Bracondale spotters' post was rendered inoperable for a while due to the fires and smoke generated around it. More historic buildings also suffered. A 500kg bomb fell on the tower of St Julian's Church on Ber Street and demolished much of the building. Further down the street, St Michael at Thorn was burnt out by fire bombs, St Paul's suffered a similar fate on Magdalen Street, as did the synagogue on Synagogue Street. A sad loss to the city in this raid were the range of old timber-framed shops that were Bond's Store and the Thatched Theatre on All Saint's Green; all were reduced to burnt-out shells by incendiary bombs.

Firebombs also rained down over the Close. Some thirty-six fire bombs fell on the Norwich School and were tackled by headmaster Theodore Acland and the boy boarders of the 'School House Fire Party', but sadly several school buildings and the Lodge could not be saved. Around the Close, fire bombs burnt out two historic properties and others were badly damaged. The story would have been a lot worse had it not been for the Fire Protection Scheme that had been put in place under Arthur Bensly Whittingham, the senior cathedral surveyor, who knew the cathedral and its precincts intimately. Whittingham had assessed vulnerable areas in the cathedral and had built fire walls and concreted and sandbagged areas accordingly to minimise the chance of fire spreading. He also raised a well-equipped and trained team of volunteer fire watchers who operated under his direction. An NFS trailer pump and crew were promptly on the scene to tackle the larger fires. They were fortunate that two canisters containing a total of 500 incendiaries failed to open and simply crashed to earth in the Close.

Another container with a further thirty-six incendiaries penetrated the roof of the cathedral transept and caused fires on the roofs and triforium but they were swiftly dealt with by the fire watchers on the roof and the NFS firemen. The worst threat was posed by sixty-one incendiaries that fell of the roofs of the north and south transepts and set it alight, but yet again, the fire watchers, Home Guard, NFS and Scout volunteers were on hand to successfully extinguish the incendiaries and the fire. By their singular and selfless actions they saved Norwich Cathedral from far worse damage, possibly even a fate akin to that of Coventry Cathedral.

The Norfolk & Norwich Hospital was peppered with incendiaries and fires broke out above the central operating theatres, two neighbouring wards and the nearby nurses' home. They had no other option than to evacuate, and nurses, staff, porters, military personnel and Civil Defence workers, soon soaking wet with water from the hoses the fire crews trained on and around the buildings, carried stretchers and assisted some 200 patients out from their initial place of safety in the cellar out of the building and onto ambulances and coaches, which evacuated them to other hospitals. Although some were shaken, not one of them suffered further injury in the process.

The City of Norwich Maternity Home in Heigham Grove was also hit by fire bombs but here there was tragedy. Warden Thomas Bright was running from the back of the building to deal with incendiaries that had fallen at the front when a high-explosive bomb detonated and he was killed by falling masonry.

Matron Miss Doris Beatrice Lane was knocked over by the blast but, finding herself uninjured, she immediately organised the patients and arranged the necessary help and evacuated them all to a place of safety. She would be recognised for her action with an MBE. The citation states: 'Miss Lane's courage, coolness and determination set an admirable example and inspired all her staff in the dangerous and difficult circumstances.' By the end of this fateful night, sixteen civilians had been killed and seventy injured.

More raids would follow at a rate of one a month for the rest of the year. As a result of the air raids on Norwich, during 1942 a total of 14,000 buildings suffered bomb damage ranging from broken windows and roof tiles to the loss of an entire wall, of which 1,200 had to be demolished. Financial and practical help came from many quarters to help get the city back on its feet. The Lord Mayor of London received over £11,000 from the Queen's Canadian Fund in May 1942, making a total at that time of £201,491 for the relief of our bombed cities, with especial donations for Bath, Norwich, York and Exeter.

The city was confronted by a huge challenge in the clearance of the bombed areas of the city, repairs and reconstruction, and compulsory powers were invoked for the first time to draft in 2,000 men from London and Birkenhead to help tackle the repairs to houses. They were joined by 250 more from London in late June. These lads really endeared themselves to the people of Norwich as they worked long days but always seemed to be cheerful. They brought their own distinctive humour with them, which worked well with the local outlook and experiences of Norwich people; they were soon affectionately known as the 'cockney sparrows'.

After the April raids many residents of Norwich feared a repetition and over the next few weeks, others whose homes were damaged left the centre of the city at dusk to stay with friends or even to sleep out in the open on Mousehold Heath. Others took to leaving their city homes at night by catching buses that would drive out into countryside areas and park up for the night so passengers could sleep and then return again in the morning.

Alderman Herbert Witard, a member of the Norwich ARP Committee, reflected:

> It was a pitiful sight to see old and young, often scantily dressed, trekking to the shelters at the sound of the siren. Young mothers with their babies and children, sick and aged seeking cover from the terror by night. There were also those who could not shelter and preferred the open country. The people who left the comfort of their homes to sleep out often in wind and rain, in fields and woods. Those who saw it can never forget the trek out of the city.
>
> Some could only walk with difficulty, children tired and crying, their mothers in great distress, many with husbands away in the forces or transferred to other places of work. In the morning, the trek back again, to work or to school. Frightened people? Yes, but frightened people helping and encouraging each other and with not a thought of surrender.

On Tuesday, 13 October 1942, HM King George VI paid a surprise visit to the city of Norwich to inspect the damage and meet some of those who had done so much to help others during the bombing of the city. All manner of personnel, from St John Ambulance and Civil Defence workers to Home Guard, nurses, Salvation Army workers, National Fire Service, police and members of the WVS, paraded in front of Norwich City Hall. Such was the secrecy surrounding the visit, many of them did not realise they were to be inspected by the king. The king paused and shared a few words with young BEM recipient, Messenger John Grix and Norwich Police Inspector Charles Buttle, who had been awarded the BEM for his work in bomb reconnaissance. His Majesty then spoke to Ruth Hardy, the MAGNA organiser. The king was unfamiliar with the MAGNA badge she wore on her Civil Defence uniform. When she explained it stood for Mutual Aid Good Neighbours' Association, the king smiled and said, 'Mrs Hardy, there is too little friendship in the world today, do keep up this wonderful work.'

It had been a year of air raid hell and the New Year Honours recognised Chief Air Raid Warden V.E. Harrison, Commander A.T. Chittock, of the Norwich City Special Constabulary, and Senior Company Officer G.N. Barrett, No. 13 (Norwich) Area NFS, with the award of an MBE. Their work was far from over.

7

THE CITY CARRIES ON
1943–44

As 1942 passed into 1943 the wartime organisations of Norwich took the chance to dust themselves down after the raids and reorganise. No. 16 Group, Royal Observer Corps, moved from their headquarters at the GPO on St Andrews to a new purpose-built centre at 'Fairfield' on Lime Tree Road. Damaged air raid wardens' and first aid posts were repaired; new posts were built to replace those that had been destroyed or severely damaged by enemy action, and more feeding centres were created. Norwich Civil Defence Services were reorganised, new posts were created where some had been destroyed or damaged beyond repair, and a purpose-built report and control centre opened on Ipswich Road.

Civil Defence Messenger Henry Hansell reminisced that the three-storey building next to the Congregational Church in Chapel Field Road East was used as accommodation for messengers on night duty. It was believed to be haunted and when the scare stories got too much they preferred to cycle up Ipswich Road to the report and control centre. Henry was sure some of the boys were more frightened of the supposed 'ghost' than they were of the bombs! He also recalled one of their favourite pastimes when things were quiet on dark nights during blackout hours, no moon or foggy nights. The boys on night duty would stand outside their base for long periods to get acclimatised to the dark. When people came out of the Theatre Royal, which was just around the corner, invariably they could not find their bearings so the boys would point them in the right direction.

In May 1943, the 10th (City of Norwich) Battalion Home Guard had increased in size to such an extent it was necessary for it to be divided into two battalions. Lower batallion numbers had already been taken by other Home Guard battalions around the county, so when the western sector was formed it became the 16th Battalion. This battalion 'did their bit' during the bombing

Norwich Girl Guide Rangers 1944. These girls cycled to bomb-damaged areas to bring blankets, food and care to air raid victims.

of Norwich in co-operation with the Civil Defence. Street fire parties were organised and commanded by Home Guards. They worked with rescue parties and provided stretcher bearers for hospitals in times of need.

Norwich suffered more damage than any other British inland city during 1942, and there was a running joke that those who came on leave or on brief breaks from London looked forward to going home for some peace and quiet. Numerous factories, shops and businesses had been lost through bombing but the city never failed to carry on. Many familiar streets looked very different, dotted as they were with public shelter signs and with their shop windows shuttered and boarded, leaving just small rectangular apertures for displays for both blast protection and to comply with the stringent blackout regulations. Others would be completely boarded up each night at dusk as shops and market stalls closed early so they too did not infringe on the blackout.

City butchers and fishmongers carried on as best they could under the strict regulations imposed by the Ministry of Food to ensure compliance with rationing. With meat in such demand, the Norwich Cattle Market saw a lot of cattle imported from Ireland. Handsome prices were commanded, dairy prices of £60 a head, bulls £32 and store cattle at £25. Meats that had been alien to the British palate also started to appear on the market such as horse, snook and whale. Restaurants were exempt from rationing, which led to a certain amount of resentment as the more affluent could supplement their food allowance by eating out. To restrict this, certain rules were put into force. No meal could cost more than 5s; no meal could consist of more than three courses; and meat and fish could not be served at the same sitting.

For those who had not managed their coupons very well, Community Feeding Centres – later renamed British Restaurants – were set up by the Ministry of Food across the country. Run by local committees on a non-profit-making basis, meals in British Restaurants came with their own restrictions. No customer could be served with a meal of more than one serving of meat, fish, game, poultry, eggs, or cheese, purchased for maximum price of 9d or less. The standard of food was very dependent on the skill of the cooks and what food was available. When all other meat sources were drying up there was always rabbit and wonders were often achieved in its creative use. The first British Restaurant in Norwich was opened by the Lord Mayor at Bull Close Schools in July 1940 and another would follow on Duke Street. Some restaurants certainly had their own sense of humour: one menu seen in Norwich, chalked on a restaurant blackboard, promised 'Sea Pie – buy it and *See* what is in it!'

Beer was not rationed either but it was in greater demand and consequently less plentiful in wartime; even less so after Morgans and Bullards breweries were bombed. Youngs, Crawshay & Youngs on King Street and Steward & Patteson, always proud to state they were 'By Appointment to the King', remained unscathed at the Pockthorpe Brewery on Barrack Street, and both worked all out so that all could still sing 'Roll Out the Barrel' with a beer in hand. They did, however, lose a number of their pubs in the air raids on the city.

On many of the Norwich streets there were now incongruous gaps between buildings where shops once stood, or long-established shops appeared in new locations after being bombed out from their previous premises. Among them was Palmer's Ironmongers, who announced they had been forced to move from St Benedict's to Magdalen Street 'on account of enemy action'.

Curl Brothers department store traded out of four premises after they were bombed: fashions, knitwear, hosiers and overalls out of the first floor of Jarrolds; dress fabrics, household linens and haberdashery from Garlands; furniture, carpets, lino, hardware and clothes for men and boys out of Westlegate; and a wholesale department on Theatre Street. Bond's on All Saint's Green hired and traded from buses, which they parked in their store car park, and a nearby corrugated building was also converted into a small restaurant serving tea and pastries.

Walking along some of the well-known streets in Norwich city centre, anyone would be struck by how some of them were free from any major bomb damage. One could bowl down London Street and it would almost appear like peacetime. Here were the city's offices of the Women's Voluntary

CURLS various Departments are now trading at the following addresses

THE OLD VALUES IN NEW SURROUNDINGS

ON JARROLDS FIRST FLOOR
(London Street)

FASHIONS, KNITWEAR, BLOUSES, &c. MILLINERY, LADIES & CHILDRENS OUT-FITTING, HOSIERY, GLOVES, OVERALLS, BELTS, RIBBONS, NECKWEAR

AT GARLANDS . . . . .

DRESS FABRICS, HOUSEHOLD LINENS, SOFT FURNISHINGS, &c., WOOLS, HABERDASHERY, &c., HANDBAGS, BOOKS, STATIONERY

AT WESTLEGATE (One minute from the old premises)

FURNITURE, CARPETS, LINO, BEDDING, CHINA, GLASS, HARDWARE, &c. MEN'S and BOYS' WEAR

CURLS WHOLESALE DEPTS.

are open at 11, Theatre Street, where good stocks have been accumulated and orders are being attended to.

CURL BROS. Ltd. The Value Centre NORWICH

LONDON ST. and WESTLEGATE   'Phone (for all Depts.) **21231**

Advert for the various departments of Curls, trading out of various premises after their store was destroyed in April 1942.

London Street viewed from near Bullen's Corner, 1944.

Castle Street looking towards London Street and Swan Lane, 1944.

Service, opened by WVS founder Lady Reading in 1942, but in those days London Street was two-way traffic and many avoided that narrow thorough-fare between the National Westminster Bank and Castle Street in the blackout after a number of very near misses, as vehicles had to pass each other and the drivers had difficulty spotting the kerb, pavement and people on it.

As London Street curved round towards the city, there was, as ever, Bullens the jewellers, with its distinctive gable end and windows that rounded the corner with Swan Lane. The wide area of the junction with Castle Street offered a useful spot for vehicles to park up and it was regularly dotted with the jeeps of personnel from the local air bases as they popped into the city.

As London Street joined Castle Street there was the International Stores grocers, with Vandykes photographic studios on the first floor, where many young servicemen or woman went for their first studio portrait in uniform, or sweethearts had a photo taken to send to their special person while they were away at war.

The Norfolk Federation of Women's Institutes was at 3 Castle Street. It was here that hundreds of girls came for their interview as prospective members of the Women's Land Army until the Norfolk WLA moved to larger premises for their county offices on Prince of Wales Road in 1941.

On Gentleman's Walk opposite the market was Joe Lyon's Tea Room, where a pleasant tea could be enjoyed in a good setting with live music and service by 'Nippies' in their smart black dresses, white aprons and starched caps. There was also H. Samuel's jewellers for sweetheart brooches on pearl and plastic backing that displayed a host of badges from all arms of the services and special gifts, and even engagement and wedding rings could be bought.

On the Haymarket there was Lipton's grocers and a fine tipple could always be obtained from the extensive stocks in the cellars of Back's, famed for having the longest bar in Norwich. The famous local 'BOP' tea was available from Lambert's shop, known as 'Ye Mecca', on the city-side corner of the Haymarket. Opposite Hay Hill was Green's men's and women's outfitters, where smart shop workers dealt courteously with customers and helped them work out which items their clothing coupons could purchase, while customers' children were kept occupied on the famous rocking horse provided for their amusement. The row ended with the elegant curve of the International Stores grocers.

But if you crossed Brigg Street on the opposite side of the Haymarket and walked to what was the smart city centre shopping area of Rampant Horse Street after the raids of 1942, you would be confronted by ruins and rubble. By 1943, however, the site of Curls' store was the scene of a highly innovative idea developed in the city whereby its basement was made watertight and used

Lipton tea dealers and the British Gas Light Company showrooms on a bustling Gentleman's Walk, 1944.

Orford Place and Red Lion Street, 1944.

as a static water reservoir containing 270,000 gallons of water to supply fire pumps in the event of another firebomb attack. The structure of the gutted Bunting's store on the corner still stood soundly because it had been built of reinforced concrete, so it was refitted as an ideally located city centre NAAFI with a tavern, large lounge, dining room and theatre ballroom.

Among the remaining bigger industries and factories, Boulton & Paul erected temporary buildings where, along with prefabricated buildings, they made a huge variety of items from Morrison air raid shelters to noses for Horsa gliders. Laurence Scott & Electromotors made electrical motors under Admiralty contracts, switchgear for submarines and controllers for tank landing craft. Motor engineers Mann Egerton built vehicles under government contracts, notably ambulances and troop carriers, and they also carried out repairs on military vehicles. Their woodworking department made over 500,000 items of furniture under government contracts during the war, while the electrical section installed air raid sirens on public buildings and installed lighting in public air raid shelters. They also went out to work on ships around the country and even installed the first radar station in the county. Busseys were appointed a Ministry of Supply Workshop for the repair of army vehicles throughout the war and a REME workshop was based in the city.

Production of Norvic footwear for men was carried out in Northampton, so it was Norvic utility footwear for women that was the main line produced in the city. Although less frequent, raids were still occurring and it was with particular sadness that, after weathering previous raids, disposing of fire bombs,

Tombland with St George's Church (left) and Erpingham Gate in the distance on the right, 1944.

Stump Cross, Magdalen Street with The Gaiety amusements arcade on the right, 1944.

clearing up and carrying on with the production of uniforms for the war effort, F.W. Harmer's was finally bombed out of its factory on St Andrews on 18 March 1943. It did eventually carry on with new premises on Havers Road.

The beautiful eighteenth-century Assembly House on Theatre Street had been used as a store and was requisitioned to become a Royal Engineers School of Camouflage. It was fortunate that the man who was to run it was Captain Oliver Messel, an artist famous for both stage sets and interior designs for notable buildings and hotels both before and after the war. He was the perfect man for the job because he also had a remarkable imagination and vision for disguising military fortifications and pillboxes as haystacks, castles, ruins and even roadside cafes.

When Messel took over the Assembly House ready to turn it into the school, he found it had been used for some time as a store. It was stacked with crates and boxes and the ceilings and walls were covered with cobwebs. However, he saw beyond that, there was still fine plaster work on the ceilings and walls, so as the structural alterations inside were made, rather than smashing out the old and replacing with utilitarian new, he ensured they were done with care and skilled plasterers on the staff used their spare time to repair the plasterwork. Paintwork was also kept in good order, even going so far as using the skills of the camouflage artists to paint many of the columns around the interior of the building in such a way that they appeared to be made from marble.

The first USAAF airmen started flying out of Norfolk in early July 1942 and thousands more would follow. Keen to introduce themselves to the community, a baseball match between the Cheyenne Broncs and the Wildcats was played at Carrow Road the same month. The first USAAF heavy bomber base in the county was opened at Shipdham in October 1942. American servicemen were soon seen on the streets and in the cafes, pubs and clubs of Norwich.

The burnt-out ruins of Harmer's clothing factory on St Andrew's after the air raid of 18 March 1943.

Inset: Pre-war advert for Harmer's showing their St Andrew's Street Works.

Dex Jordan and Charlie Young, 7th Bombardment Squadron, 34th Bombardment Group, 8th USAAF, outside City Hall, Norwich, August 1944.

For some local people they were too brash and flash, and it would take quite some adjustment for the Americans to understand just how long Britain had been at war and the depravation the country had suffered because of it. Local girls started to take a shine to these well-mannered and very smart young servicemen, who had the money to buy them gifts and access the likes of chocolates, tinned foods and nylon stockings that were not readily available under wartime shortages. Some fathers forbade their daughters associating with American servicemen and some jealousies erupted, especially if a local servicemen came home on leave to discover his girlfriend had forsaken him for a 'Yank'.

A sea change was needed. A guide had been produced for American servicemen coming to Britain, instructional sessions and leaflets offered a range of 'Dos and Don'ts' and an information film was produced to help American servicemen understand more about British culture and how the war had affected us. Once a little time had passed, things settled down and the natural curiosity of many Norfolk people and the warmth and good manners of the American servicemen saw many enduring friendships emerge. The thousands of American service personnel were soon regarded as 'the Friendly Invasion'.

American servicemen were invited to spend Christmas at hundreds of Norwich homes and brought all sorts of treats such as chocolate bars and even whole turkeys and cranberry sauce in tins. In return, hundreds of Norwich children were entertained at Christmas parties on nearby bases. In a particularly kind gesture, the British War Relief Society of the United States and Junior Red Cross sent thousands gifts to Norwich City Hall for distribution to local children.

By mid-1944 the Eighth Air Force had grown to become the biggest military air fleet ever seen, with a total of 122 bases, 200,000 personnel, 2,000 four-engine bombers and 1,000 fighter aircraft, and entered into history as the 'Mighty Eighth'. From late 1942, base after base opened across the county. Two American Air Divisions had bases in Norfolk, with a total of eighteen USAAF airfields across the county. The 2nd Air Division had the largest presence, predominantly flying Consolidated B-24 Liberators. Mass formations of Liberator aircraft became a regular sight in the skies over and near the city. Phil Cooper, the editor of the *Norwich Union Magazine*, wrote:

> Norwich itself was surrounded by American 'dromes that no matter which way the wind lay, Liberators were constantly taking off over our very rooftops. In the winter mornings long before dawn the Libs provided an amazing spectacle, not only with their navigation lights, by reason of the multi-coloured flares they dropped in the course of assuming their formations.

There were fourteen USAAF bases within a 30-mile radius of Norwich that accommodated a total force of over 50,000 personnel. American servicemen on short leave passes loved to come to Norwich. Officers usually managed to wangle their own transport in the form of a jeep, which they would share with their brother officers and air crew team.

Some parked wherever they could on the city streets but the preferred parking lot was on waste ground at the junction of Whitefriars and Barrack Street, which allowed easy access for the American Red Cross Club and the Samson and Hercules ballroom. Many city youngsters in that area knew where the Americans parked and hung around during the day at weekends and early evenings, greeting the Americans with the question, 'Got any gum, chum?' The hope being to cadge some chewing gum or sweets, perhaps even earning a tip helping with directions or even running a message to a local sweetheart to let her know her boy was 'in town'.

Most of the enlisted men of the USAAF ended up on the crowded 'liberty trucks' that regularly ran the men from the bases to the city and disgorged their passengers on the Cattle Market. Some liked to go dancing to the music of Eddie Gates, Dolly Bridges or stomping to Billie Duncan and his jitterbug jive band at the Lido. Others went for an evening in one of the city's many pubs where they were introduced to new games such as darts, which they seemed to find hilarious when they first encountered it. They also found fish and chips out of newspaper quite a novel experience all round. The Bell on Orford Hill was always popular with the USAAF lads and the Duke of Connaught on Prince of Wales Road drew black servicemen through its doors. Segregation was still practised in the American military forces, but to the credit of Norwich people, they never could see the point in it and all were welcome.

At Blackfriars Hall there were basketball matches and boxing, concerts were staged regularly at a variety of venues around the city or the Americans could take in a movie at cinemas like the Regent on Prince of Wales Road, Theatre de Luxe on St Andrew's or the Haymarket. There were shows at the Theatre Royal or at the YMCA on St Giles, where free concerts were given on Sunday evenings.

The preferred venue for USAAF visitors to Norwich for meeting girls and dancing soon became the Samson and Hercules ballroom. Teddy Bush, owner of the Sam and Herc – otherwise known as 'the muscle men' after the two carved figures either side of the door, – was keen to welcome the business of American servicemen and laid on American-style music with popular Norwich-born dance band leader Gerry Hoey and his band three nights a week. They certainly had a surprise when Major Glenn Miller and the Army

Air Force band dropped in to play during their month-long tour of the East Anglian air bases in June 1944.

For those on only an evening pass, the 'liberty trucks' would depart at 11 p.m., and woe betide the men who missed them. There were always plenty of American Military Policemen in their distinctive white helmets that earned them the nickname 'Snowdrops' to pick up stragglers and deal with any trouble.

Entrance to 'Sam and Herc' ballroom on Tombland that was so popular with 8th USAAF service personnel on a night out in Norwich.

For those on day passes, many just enjoyed a day exploring the historic sites of the city and visiting shops. They also enjoyed our museums and the parks at Eaton and Earlham provided lovely places for a stroll. The American Red Cross Service Club was set up in the shadow of the cathedral at the Bishop's Palace and US servicemen were provided with dormitories for their visits in the city at 13, The Close and at an annex on Bethel Street. Often 120,000 men and women passed through the club in a single month, with up to a thousand staying in the city overnight. Even with just fleeting visits, life was lived fast in wartime and many a wartime romance blossomed between Norwich girls and American servicemen. Quite a few local girls went back Stateside with their husbands after the war, while some were widowed before their life together got started.

Norwich also had occasional visits from one of the best-known USAAF pilots in the world, none other than Hollywood film star Major James M. 'Jimmy' Stewart, who came to Tibenham as 703rd Squadron Commander with the 445th Bombardment Group and flew on numerous missions from the base. In March 1944, he was promoted and transferred to the 453rd Bombardment Group at Old Buckenham as their group executive officer. This was a new B-24 unit that had been experiencing difficulties, so to inspire confidence in these men Stewart flew as command pilot in the lead aircraft on numerous missions deep into Nazi-occupied Europe. When Stewart flew operations, his reputation was for hitting the target and bringing back crews alive. He never courted attention and conducted himself as just another officer of the USAAF. Jimmy was both well liked and respected by his comrades and returned to Norfolk for their reunions over the years after the war. In a feature tribute to Stewart by Colonel Beirne Lay Junior in the US paper *The Saturday Evening Post* of 15 December 1945, just two blots on his record were related:

When it came to driving a jeep, he was the worst navigator in England. Once he got lost driving from Tibenham to wing headquarters, a distance of five miles. On a more ambitious effort, from London to Norwich, he finally pulled up in Birmingham.

A formation of 467th Bomb Group B-24 Liberators flying over Norwich on Christmas Eve, 1944.

The men of the Mighty Eighth in East Anglia flew mission after mission, often in daylight and deep over enemy territory. Roland Campbell, who also flew with 445th Bomb Group out of Tibenham, recalled:

> We had two other enemies during the war besides the Germans. The first was the British anti-aircraft gunners, who would occasionally shoot at us. The second enemy was the terrible English weather. We were constantly plagued with fog and overcast skies. Sometimes returning to our base we would find only a 75' to 100' cloud ceiling, which made it very difficult to find our base and avoid collision with other aircraft.

It was a problem common to all pilots but one that led to a number of tragic accidents over the war years, and one remains in the memories of Norwich people above all others. It was 24 November 1944 and 20-year-old pilot Second Lieutenant Ralph J. Dooley and his crew from 753rd Squadron, 458th Bomb Group had flown out from their airfield at Horsham St Faith on a training mission aboard the B-24 Liberator *Lady Jane*. At approximately 1700 they were flying low when they suddenly encountered low cloud and Dooley attempted to pull up and out of it. Brian Gray was a 9 years old, playing with his friends on a bomb site between Browne Street and Portway Place off Old Palace Road when they spotted the plane:

> As it passed over our heads towards Heigham Road it banked round and a wing hit one of the pinnacles on the tower of St Phillip's Church. Half of the wing and one engine finished up in the trees in the churchyard.
> The plane then came back over our heads, just missing Dereham Road Baptist Church. It flew one wing up, one down and crashed into the corporation yard at the end of Barker Street off Heigham Street, sending up a cloud of black smoke.

It was clear to all who witnessed the tragedy that Dooley gave his life to save those of the people in the built-up area below him. Several wrote on behalf of their neighbourhood and personally to the base commander to praise the selfless act of the pilot. One lady told how she had seen the incident:

> I had just left the Lazar House on Sprowston Road and noticed the bomber flying very low. At first I did not realise any danger, so fascinated was I in watching the skill of the pilot and his efforts to gain height. A girl just passing me with a pram screamed 'It's coming down'. Snatching her baby out the pram, she went up an opening, leaving the pram to trundle into the gutter. I uttered a silent prayer for its safe landing and a thank you to the crew.

It was only later that she learned of the loss of the aircraft and all crew. A plaque commemorating the men was erected on houses near the crash site. The houses have since been demolished and the plaque has been removed to flats nearby but a small commemorative service is held there every year.

The last air raid on Norwich took place on 6 November 1943, but that was not the end of the deadly German aerial menace for Norwich. The V2 was a long-range rocket known in Germany as the *Vergeltungswaffe 2* retaliation weapon. London was the main target, although 'short falls' of V weapons could occur over much of south-east England, but there were other targets including Norwich. Operated by Versuchs Artillerie Batterie 444 under the command of Oberst Gerhard Stegmeier, the launch site for the attacks on the city was in a wood near Rijs in Southwest Friesland, in the Netherlands.

Less than a year after the last bomb was dropped on Norwich, the first V2 launched against the city fell on a field near Ranworth at 4.25 p.m. on 26 September 1944, causing a great explosion and crater and sending a column

Plaque erected in memory of Lieutenant Ralph J. Dooley and the crew of B-24 'Lady Jane', who sacrificed their lives rather than crash into houses on Barker Street on 24 November 1944.

of smoke 2,000ft in the air. The only casualty was a man who required treatment for shock after the blast. More rockets followed and in some cases damage was caused, people were injured and there were many narrow escapes, but by some miracle no one was killed in any of the V2 landings on the county and Norwich never received a hit by a V2.

The rocket that came closest to the city crashed on the Royal Norwich Golf Club course at Hellesdon on 3 October 1944. On that day, Reg Ford was a young man enjoying one of his visits to the Theatre de Luxe, a cinema often referred to simply as 'The Ranch' because it always seemed to be showing western films. He was such a regular he had got friendly with 'Big Jock' the doorman:

I sat there and they called the siren and up on the screen that says would you like to leave the theatre or would you like to stop and I took a chance and stopped. Raids, I been in some raids but I never heard a bang like that, and then all of a sudden the siren all clear went. I watched the end of the film and when I come out and I said to old Jock, 'What the hell was that, the whole screen moved,' and he said, you know how things travelled in them days, there weren't no television then, and he say they reckon that was a rocket or something dropped up on the golf links.

He was right and it left a crater 33ft by 37ft and 12ft deep. Golfers would joke it was the biggest bunker on the course! The blast caused minor damage to some 400 homes in the area between Dereham Road and Boundary. Thankfully, nobody was killed but an elderly lady was treated for shock. This was undoubtedly a sobering near miss; if any of the V2s had hit its target the story would have been very different. The last V2 aimed at Norwich fell on a field at Manor Farm, Ingworth, on 12 October 1944, causing minor damage to twenty-four houses and the church.

Norwich had endured 1,443 alerts since the first wail of the sirens on the day war broke out, an average of one a day over the next four years. Approximately 680 HE and over 25,000 incendiary bombs had fallen on the city in forty-four raids that killed 340 people and injured over 1,000. Some 2,651 homes had been seriously damaged, indeed a total of 30,354 houses had suffered damage to a greater or lesser extent out of the total number of 35,569 in the city.

8

VICTORY

After the successful progress of the Allies after the D-Day landings in June 1944 the need for the Home Guard diminished rapidly. On 30 August 1944 the War Office issued instructions for standing down the Home Guard, and a formal notice circulated in October gave notification that it was to stand down from active duties in November 1944. A stand down parade and march past of Norwich City Home Guard past City Hall took place on 3 December 1944.

Norwich greeted 1945 with new confidence and it was announced on 6 January 1945 that the city had officially honoured the Royal Norfolk Regiment by granting it the Freedom of the City and with that the privilege of marching through the city with colours flying, band playing and bayonets fixed. People dared to see a glimmer of light at the end of the tunnel, a light of victory for the Allies.

One good bit of news was that there was to be some home leave for service personnel from the Continent. The national newspapers were quick to pick up on the first five of 'Monty's ATS', who had been part of the first contingent of 18 ATS that had landed in France in June 1944, were to return on leave, among them one 'Red Cap' Military Policewoman, our very own Joyce 'Joe' Collins of Beverley Road.

For our lads in 1st Battalion, the Royal Norfolk Regiment and the Norfolk Yeomanry, there was still some hard fighting to be done as they fought to cross the Rhine in March and advanced into Germany. The 2nd Battalion had gone through hell at Kohima in 1944 and suffered terrible casualties. It was rebuilding again in the early months of 1945 and was withdrawn from Burma on 13 April 1945 and flown to India. It arrived at Calcutta on 18 April to prepare for the new offensive on Rangoon in May. It should not be forgotten there were also many Norwich servicemen in corps and other regiments serving in these campaigns too; indeed there were Norwich men and women serving

Gentleman's Walk packed with people celebrating VE Day on 8 May 1945.

all over the world in all three services and support organisations such as the
NAAFI, ENSA, Red Cross and Salvation Army.

By April it was not if but when the war would end in favour of the Allies,
and Alan Plume, the new Chief Constable of Norwich, although pretty much
a teetotaller himself, was keen to state publicly there had been enough 'do
this and do that' in wartime and suggested that the pubs of the city should cut
down their opening hours to preserve stocks of beer and to make sure they
were ready to be open all day to celebrate when final victory was achieved.
He did add that he hoped the good citizens of the city would only drink in
moderation. Victory in Europe was announced on 8 May 1945, and neighbours
clubbed together to gather funds, sufficient food coupons, tables, chairs, cloths
and bunting to stage street parties.

There were no formal plans for the city centre but thousands gathered there,
some carrying flags to celebrate the occasion. There was hugging and kissing,
impromptu sing-songs and – as if we had not had enough bangs – some wags
started letting off fireworks in the street.

A formal victory thanksgiving march past of many forces and wartime
organisations was staged at City Hall led by bands of the Dorset Regiment and
the USAAF, followed by a service at the cathedral on Sunday, 13 May. For many
families, these celebrations were only fleeting as many loved ones had still not

VE Day revellers clear some space as impromptu fireworks are let off in Norwich City Centre, 8 May 1945.

returned from the war in Europe. Indeed, those who happened to be on leave at the time of VE Day had to return to their units and, in some cases, it would be months before they would be 'demobbed' and return to civvy street.

Meanwhile, the men in the Far East, often known as 'the forgotten army' (and they felt this when they heard of such events back home), were fighting an all too real war in the jungles of India and Burma, while others endured captivity in Japanese hands until the Japanese surrendered and at last they could celebrate VJ Day on 2 September 1945. Within days it was announced the first prisoners were on their way back from captivity in the Far East. Among those released was Miss Mabel Constance Baggs (47), a Norwich-born Church Mission Society missionary, who had been in Japan for the past seven years and had chosen to stay there when Japan declared war. Held at a Tokyo internment camp, she never lost her spirit and was described by fellow internees as 'the life and soul of the party'. She carried on her missionary work in Japan until 1963 and remained a committed Christian until she died in 1984.

Three battalions of the Royal Norfolk Regiment had been in Japanese hands since the fall of Singapore and hundreds of them had died while in captivity as they were forced to labour on the infamous Burma–Siam Railway in Thailand or down the mines on mainland Japan. Beaten, denied access to medical supplies or reasonable food and in some cases subjected to torture, they had suffered terrible ulcers and tropical diseases such as malaria and dysentery. These men had gone through hell but they never forgot they were soldiers.

When the camps were liberated it was painfully clear that many of those who had been prisoners of war in Japanese hands were in bad shape, some reduced to living skeletons. British authorities would not let them come home immediately, insisting instead they spent some time in rest and recuperation (and fattening up) in Canada. For many of them and those who had served in the Far East in general, they would not get home until 1946 and they would never have the chance to take part in a victory parade. Many would reflect years later, 'we were just grateful to be alive and get home'.

Families back in Norwich eagerly anticipated the return of their loved ones. Many others had to come to terms with the realisation that their son, dad or brother would not be coming home again. For those who had lost their homes in the bombing there were prefab houses all over the city and its suburbs. Some folks had a prefab as their first marital home and chose to live in them for the rest of their lives, while other areas were redeveloped into new housing estates. Meanwhile, some parts of the city remained bomb sites, played on by local children for decades afterwards.

The Norwich City Plan for the reconstruction of the city published in 1945 suggested vast amounts of modernisation. Thank goodness the wide-open vistas and modern boulevards of the plan were not all carried out, although it has seemed over the years that city planners have committed their own acts of destruction where the Luftwaffe failed. Today we still have our fine city, its remaining historical buildings standing cheek by jowl with the modern. It works, it is a very special place. Best we look after it.

NORWICH CIVIL DEFENCE ORGANISATION 1942

First Aid Posts & Cleansing Stations
Norfolk & Norwich Hospital; Sussex St ARP Headquarters (entrance Bakers Rd);
Colman Road School; Stuart School, Telegraph Lane

Cleansing Stations
Angel Road School
Lakenham School
Duke Street School

Emergency Feeding Centres
Angel Road Senior Girls' School; Heigham House School, West Pottergate; Bull
Close Infants' School, Bull Close Rd; Catton Grove Primary School, Peterson Rd;
Blyth Secondary School, Constitution Hill; Larkman Lane Senior School, Clarkson
Rd; Anguish's Housecraft School, Hall Rd; Wensum View Senior School, Waterworks
Rd; Cavell Primary School, Duckett Cl; Willow Lane Primary School; Alderman Jex
Senior Boys' School, Colman Road; Open Air School, South Park Ave; Sprowston Rd;
Dowson Senior Girls' School, Valpy Ave

Rest Centres
Angel Road School; Heigham House School, West Pottergate; Bignold School,
Crooks Pl; Lakenham Council School, City Rd; Catton Grove School, Middleton
Cl; Larkman Lane School, Clarkson Rd; Colman Road School, South Park Ave;
Mousehold Avenue School; Crome & Stuart Schools, Telegraph Lane; Norman
School, Peterson Rd; George White School, Silver Rd; Wellesley Avenue School

British Restaurants
Bull Close School, Bull Close Rd
Duke Street School

Information Centres
Citizens Advice Bureau
City hall
Main Centre:
> Central Library, St Andrews St

Branch Centres:
> Lazar House Branch Library, Sprowston Rd
> Earlham Branch Library, Colman Rd
> Mile Cross Library, Aylsham Rd
> Thorpe Branch Library, Plumstead Rd

Civil Defence Wardens' Service
List of posts (Norwich unless otherwise stated)
Chief Warden's office
Fire Guard office
Division 1 Headquarters,:11 West Parade
Subsidiary Depot: 1 Rackham Rd
Operational Headquarters: Heigham Grove Report Centre

Group 'A'
A1 Rackham Rd; A4 Woodcock Road, near Catton Grove Rd; A2 Sun Lane
Secondary School, Roseberry Rd; A5 Bullard Close; A3 Harmer Rd

Group 'E'
E1 19 St Stephens Rd; E6 Fairfield Rd, near Town Close Rd; E4 Sigismund Rd by
Trafford Rd; E7 Eaton Rd by Waverley Rd, Eaton

Group 'F'
F1 Trory St; F5 Newmarket Rd, Eagle Public House; F2 Bignold School, Essex St
; F6 Christ Church Ave, Eaton; F3 Cambridge St; F7 Judges Walk by Unthank Rd,
Eaton; F4 Newmarket St by Bury St; F8 9 Eaton Hill, Eaton

Group 'G'
G1 Clarendon Steps; G6 The Avenues by Christ Church Rd; G2 Warwick St; G7
Lubbock Close by Elizabeth Fry Rd, Eaton; G4 Milford Rd; G8 Colman Rd,
Eaton; G5 Muriel Rd, Eaton

Group 'H'
H1 60 West Pottergate; H5 St Barnabas, Russell St; H2 Gladstone St by Stafford St;
H6 Barker St; H3 St Thomas Rd; H7 Nelson Street School; H4 45 Dereham Rd;
H8 Turner Rd, Orphanage Home

Group 'J'
J2 Dereham Rd by Larkman Ln, Costessey; J4 Earlham Grove, Eaton; J3 Gilbard
Rd, Eaton; J5 Gipsy Lane/Bowthorpe Rd

Group 'K'
K1 Aylsham Rd opp Waterloo Pk (K7 sub-Post); K5 Civic Gardens by Rye Ave; K2 Shorncliffe Ave; K6 Mile Cross Rd/Aylsham Rd; K3 Drayton Rd by Wheeler Rd; K7 Wensum Park, St Martins Rd; K4 Peterson Rd

Group Centre: Dowson School, Valpy Ave
Division 2 Headquarters: 23 Red Lion St
Subsidiary Depot: 3 Milverton Rd
Operational Headquarters: Old Report Centre, Market Place

Group 'B'
B1 George White School, Silver Rd; B4 Gertrude ; B3 Sprowston Rd/Wall Rd – B6 Mousehold Infants' School, Lavengro Rd

Group 'C'
C2 Clarence Rd by Carrow Rd; C5 Lion Wood Rd by Plumstead Rd; C3 Chalk Hill Works, Rosary Rd; C6 Heathside Rd by Cotman Rd; C4 Playground, Wolfe Rd; C7 Britannia Rd, opp. Vincent Rd

Group 'D'
D2 Cricket Ground Rd; D4 Ber Street Gates; D3 Long John Hill by Barrett Rd; D5 Southwell Rd by Hall Rd

Group 'M'
M1 Tombland; M5 Sussex St; M2 Palace Plain; M6 Duke St; M3 Charlton Rd; M7 Botolph St; M4 Bull Cl; M8 Heath Rd

Group Centre: St Saviours Hall, St Saviours Ln

Group 'O'
O1 2 Market Pl (Guildhall Hill); O4 Thorn Ln; O1 Market Pl (Action Station); O5 Loyalty Court, St Stephens St; O2 St Gregory's Alley; O6 Bloomsbury Pl, Rose Ln; O3 Three Kings Ln; O7 Queens Rd adj. Victoria Station Coal Yard

Auxiliary Fire Stations

Bethel Street; Barrack Street/Steward & Patteson's Garage; Chapel Field Road/ St Stephen's Back Street; Silver Road/Old Tram Sheds; Sayer Street/Midland Street; Mousehold Lane/Grange & Samuels Builder's Yard; Prince of Wales Road/Oil Mills Yard; The Gothics, Hall Road

APPENDIX 2

NORWICH AIR RAID CASUALTIES DURING THE SECOND WORLD WAR

Details reproduced by kind permission of the Commonwealth War Graves Commission

ACTON, JAMES GREENWOOD, 7 May 1942. Age 76. 53 The Avenues, Norwich. Injured 27 April 1942, at 53 The Avenues; died at St Michael's Buildings, Aylsham.

ALDEN, MAY BLANCHE, 29 April 1942. Age 60. 4 Home Street, Heigham Street. Widow of Isaac John Alden. Died at Raynham Street.

ALDOUS, CHARLES, 28 April 1942. Age 74. 43 Cherry Street. Died at The Lodge, Bowthorpe Road.

AMES, DAISY, 27 April 1942. Age 50. 3 Bixfields Buildings, Rupert Street. Daughter of Ellen and of the late Thomas Ames. Died at 3 Bixfields Buildings.

AMES, ELLEN, 27 April 1942. Age 81. 3 Bixfields Buildings, Rupert Street. Daughter of the late Mr and Mrs Fisher; widow of Thomas Ames. Died at 3 Bixfields Buildings.

AUSTIN, EPHRAIM, 7 May 1942. Age 84. Husband of the late Frances Elizabeth Austin. Died of shock as a result of the April bombing, at The Lodge, Bowthorpe Road.

BACK, HILDA MARY, 29 April 1942. Age 54. FAP member. Daughter of E.H. Back, 5A Earlham Road, and of the late Rev. Arthur James Back. Died at 5A Earlham Road.

BACON, CHARLES HENRY, 9 July 1940. Age 36. 40 Pilling Park Road, Plumstead. Died at Boulton & Paul's Works.

BALAAM, MAUD PAMELA, 9 July 1940. Age 40. Daughter of Edith Balaam, 7 St John's Terrace, Ashbourne Street and of the late Walter Balaam. Died at Carrow Hill.

BALES, WILLIAM GEORGE, 1 August 1940. Age 32. 22 Chapel Street. Son of Mr and Mrs A. Bales, 12 Henderson Road. Died at Boulton & Paul's Works.

BARBER, ALFRED GEOFFREY, 28 April 1942. Age 32. 55 Livingstone Street. Son of Henry and Eliza Emma Barber. Injured at 55 Livingstone Street; died same day at The Lodge, Bowthorpe Road.

BARBER, ELIZA EMMA, 30 April 1942. Age 64. 55 Livingstone Street. Wife of Henry Barber. Died at 55 Livingstone Street.

BARBER, HENRY, 30 April 1942. Age 67. 55 Livingstone Street. Husband of Eliza Emma Barber. Died at 55 Livingstone Street.

BARKWAY, CAROLINE MARY ANN, 1 May 1942. Age 89. 143 Rosary Road. Widow of Charles Barkway. Injured 29 April 1942, at 143 Rosary Road; died at Thorpe Hamlet first aid post.

BELDING, KENNETH GEORGE, 5 September 1942. Age 25. Son of Mr and Mrs Belding, of 11 St David's Place, Park Road, Hendon, Middlesex; husband of Vera Belding, of 187 Essex Street. Died at Frazer's Joinery Works.

BELL, HARRIET, 3 May 1942. Age 64. 421 Dereham Road, Norwich. Daughter of Mr and Mrs T. Chaplin of Garvestone, widow of William Bell. Injured 27 April 1942, at 421 Dereham Road; died at Hellesdon Hospital.

BELL, LEONARD PERCY, 1 August 1940. Age 45. Husband of May Lucy Bell, 56 Cardiff Road. Died at Goods Yard, Thorpe Station.

BETTS, CLARE, 27 April 1942. Age 63. 8 Helena Road. Husband of Nellie Betts. Died at 8 Helena Road.

BETTS, NELLIE, 27 April 1942. Age 63. 8 Helena Road. Wife of Clare Betts. Died at 8 Helena Road.

BLOGG, GLADYS VIOLET, 28 April 1942. Age 47. 47 Elm Grove Lane. Daughter of the late Alexander and Hannah Rudling; wife of Sidney Albert Blogg. Died at 47 Elm Grove Lane.

BLOGG, SIDNEY ALBERT, 28 April 1942. Age 48. 47 Elm Grove Lane. Son of the late Arthur Blogg; husband of Gladys Violet Blogg. Died at 47 Elm Grove Lane.

BLOMFIELD, LAURA, 27 June 1942. Age 84. 16 Cotman Road. Daughter of the late Mr and Mrs James Warner, of White House, Scarning; widow of Edward Mills Blomfield. Died at 16 Cotman Road.

BOWDEN, WILLIAM THOMAS, 29 April 1942. Age 49. Son of Peter Thomas Bowden, 8 Banksome Road; husband of Rosina Victoria Bowden, of the same address. Died at 121A Newmarket Road.

BOWERS, MORRIS, 28 April 1942. Age 84. The Lodge, Bowthorpe Road. Husband of the late Betsy Bishop Bowers. Died at The Lodge, Bowthorpe Road.

BRACEY, ARTHUR CYRIL, 1 August 1940. Age 24. Son of A.A. and E.F. Bracey, 25 Leonard Street, St Augustine's; husband of D.E. Bracey, of 9 Caston Road, Thorpe-next-Norwich. Died at Boulton & Paul's Works.

BRAMBLE, GWENDOLINE MARGARET, 30 July 1940. Age 3. 6 Victoria Terrace, Horns Lane. Daughter of Gunner Harold John Bramble, RA, and Phyllis Mildred Bramble. Died at 6 Victoria Terrace.

BRAMBLE, JILL JOCELYN, 30 July 1940. Aged 17 months; of 6 Victoria Terrace, Horns Lane. Daughter of Gunner Harold John Bramble, RA, and Phyllis Mildred Bramble. Died at 6 Victoria Terrace.

BRAMBLE, PETER JOHN, 30 July 1940. Age 5. 6 Victoria Terrace, Horns Lane. Son of Gunner Harold John Bramble, RA, and Phyllis Mildred Bramble. Injured at 6 Victoria Terrace; died same day at Norfolk and Norwich Hospital.

BRAMBLE, PHYLLIS MILDRED, 30 July 1940. Age 26. 6 Victoria Terrace, Horns Lane. Daughter of Frederick Arthur and Margaret Elizabeth Blomfield, of 2 Wales Square, Prince of Wales Road; wife of Gunner Harold John Bramble, RA. Injured 30 July 1940, at 6 Victoria Terrace; died same day at Norfolk and Norwich Hospital.

BRIDGES, EDITH VIOLET, 30 July 1940. Age 34. 1 Lorne Place, Argyle Street. Wife of A.E. Bridges. Died at 1 Lorne Place.

BRIGHT, THOMAS VICTOR, 27 June 1942. Age 55. Air Raid Warden. Son of Ellen Bright, of Cambridge, and the late William Bright; husband of Mabel Annie Hayward Bright, of 53 Mill Hill Road. Died at Maternity Home, Heigham Grove.

BRIGHTON, BESSIE ALICE, 28 April 1942. Age 36. 71 Belvoir Street. Wife of Corporal George Patrick Brighton, RAF. Died at 71 Belvoir Street.

BRIGHTON, DOROTHY ALICE, 29 April 1942. Age 32. 16 Ethel Road, Thorpe. Daughter of Mr and Mrs J.T. Day, of Ethel Cottage, Whapload, Lowestoft, Suffolk; wife of Herbert (Howard) Brighton. Died at Ethel Road shelter.

BRIGHTON, ENID SHEILA, 28 April 1942. Age 3. 71 Belvoir Street. Daughter of Corporal George Patrick Brighton, RAF, and Bessie Alice Brighton. Died at 71 Belvoir Street.

BRIGHTON, HERBERT HOWARD, 29 April 1942. Age 35. Home Guard, 16 Ethel Road, Thorpe. Son of Mr and Mrs L.H. Brighton, of 9 Beatrice Road, Thorpe; husband of Dorothy Alice Brighton. Died at Ethel Road Shelter.

BRIGHTON, PETER GEORGE, 28 April 1942. Age 11. 71 Belvoir Street. Son of Corporal George Patrick Brighton, RAF, and Bessie Alice Brighton. Died at 71 Belvoir Street.

BRITCHER, EDWARD JOHN, 7 May 1941. Age 15. 47 Cadge Close. Son of Edward Joseph and Ethel Maud Britcher. Died at 47 Cadge Close.

BRITCHER, EDWARD JOSEPH, 7 May 1941. Age 41. 47 Cadge Close. Husband of Ethel Maud Britcher. Died at 47 Cadge Close.

BRITCHER, ETHEL MAUD, 8 May 1941. Age 37. 47 Cadge Close. Wife of Edward Joseph Britcher. Injured 7 May 1941, at 47 Cadge Close; died at Norfolk and Norwich Hospital.

BRITCHER, IRENE VIOLET, 7 May 1941. Age 10. 47 Cadge Close. Daughter of Edward Joseph and Ethel Maud Britcher. Died at 47 Cadge Close.

BRITCHER, LEONARD CYRIL, 7 May 1941. Age 13. 47 Cadge Close. Son of Edward Joseph and Ethel Maud Britcher. Died at 47 Cadge Close.

BROOKS, CHARLES ERNEST, 9 July 1940. Age 39. Husband of Elsie May Brooks, 11 Prospect Road. Died at Boulton & Paul's Works.

BROWN, HILDA MARY, 1 August 1940. Age 41. Wife of Joseph Brown, 103 Barrett Road, Lakenham. Died at Iron Works.

BRUFF, WILLIAM BERTRAM, 2 August 1942. Age 54. 28 York Street. Son of the late Benjamin and Henrietta Bruff. Died at Gunton Sons and Dyball's premises, St George Street.

BRUNNING, ROSA EDITH, 2 December 1940. Age 31. 47 St John Street. Daughter of E.G. Freeman; wife of Corporal William Bullock Brunning, RAF (killed in same incident). Died at 47 St John Street.

BRYANT, DEREK ARTHUR, Flight Sergeant, RAF, 28 April 1942. Age 27. Son of Albert James Bryant and Amy Isabel Bryant, Thorpe St Andrew.

BUCK, CHARLES STEPHEN. Age 67. 2 Boundary Road, Hellesdon. Son of the late Stephen and Ann Buck. Died at 2 Boundary Road.

BUCK, THOMAS ROBERT, 2 May 1942. Age 69. 52 Patteson Road, Norwich, Norfolk. Died at White Lodge Emergency Hospital, Exning.

BURR, BERTIE WILLIAM, 28 April 1942. Age 51. Fire watcher. Husband of May Burr, 122 Gipsy Lane. Injured at Oak Street; died same day at Norfolk and Norwich Hospital.

BURRELL, JOHN WILLIAM, 4 May 1942. Age 85. 23 Paddock Street, Norwich. Husband of the late Emily Burrell. Injured at The Lodge, Bowthorpe Road, Norwich; died at St Michael's Buildings, Aylsham.

BURRELL, MAUD ETHEL, 12 July 1940. Age 37. Daughter of Mr and Mrs W. Burrell, 21 Mansfield Lane. Injured 9 July 1940 at Norwich; died at Norfolk and Norwich Hospital.

BURTON, CLARA, 29 April 1942. Age 54. 46 Alexandra Road. Wife of Ernest John Burton. Died at 46 Alexandra Road.

BURTON, ERNEST JOHN, 29 April 1942. Age 56. 46 Alexandra Road. Husband of Clara Burton. Died at 46 Alexandra Road.

BURTON, JOHN ERNEST FRANK, 29 April 1942. Age 19. 46 Alexandra Road. Son of Ernest John and Clara Burton. Died at 46 Alexandra Road.

BURTON, SYBIL CONSTANCE, 29 April 1942. Age 13. 46 Alexandra Road. Daughter of Ernest John and Clara Burton. Died at 46 Alexandra Road.

BUSH, ANTHONY DAVID, 30 April 1942. Age 4. Son of Charles Robert and Gladys Mary Bush. Died at The Lodge, Bowthorpe Road.

BUSSEY, SAM, 28 April 1942. Age 39. Senior Company Officer, NFS. Son of James and Alice Bussey, 5 Chapel Lane, Shaw, Lancashire; husband of Norah Mary Bussey, 4 Flat, Fire Station, Bethel Street. Died at Oak Street.

BUTCHER, ARTHUR, 27 April 1942. Age 62. 2 Bixfields Buildings, Rupert Street. Husband of Beatrice Louisa Butcher. Died at 2 Bixfields Buildings.

BUTCHER, BEATRICE LOUISA, 27 April 1942. Age 62. 2 Bixfields Buildings, Rupert Street. Wife of Arthur Butcher. Died at 2 Bixfields Buildings.

BUTLER, GEORGE WALTER, 28 April 1942. Age 44. ARP Rescue Service. Son of Walter Butler and the late Emma Butler, 12 Barker Street; husband of Una Mary Butler, 21 Civic Gardens. Injured at Oak Street, died same day at 21 Civic Gardens.

BUXTON, CHRISTOPHER LAST, 28 April 1942. Age 33. Son of John and Alice Buxton, Red House, Botesdale, Bury St Edmunds, Suffolk; husband of Gladys May Buxton, 4 Council Houses, Thurston, Bury St Edmunds. Died at 22 Northumberland Street.

CAREY, VIOLET MARY, 27 April 1942. Age 70. 79 Northcote Road. Died at 79 Northcote Road.

CAREY, WALTER ROBERT, 27 April 1942. Age 70. 79 Northcote Road. Died at 79 Northcote Road.

CARR, CAROLINE MARY, 29 April 1942. Age 85. Elvina, Clabon Close, Wall Road. Widow of George Walter Carr. Died at Clabon Close.

CARR, ELLEN KATHLEEN, 1 August 1940. Age 17. Daughter of Arthur James and Emily Rosetta Carr, 32 Argyle Street. Died at Boulton & Paul's Works.

CARTER, META VIOLET, 28 April 1942. Age 41. 142 Drayton Road. Daughter of Mr and Mrs N.J. Lean, 1 Waterloo Terrace, Truro, Cornwall; wife of Lieutenant G.F. Carter, Pioneer Corps. Injured 27 April 1942, at 142 Drayton Road; died at Wardens' Post, Drayton Road.

CATCHPOLE, SIDNEY MAURICE, 27 April 1942. Age 12. 23 Bacon Road. Son of G. Catchpole and William Thomas Catchpole. Died at 23 Bacon Road.

CATCHPOLE, WILLIAM THOMAS, 27 April 1942. Age 47. 23 Bacon Road. Husband of G. Catchpole. Died at 23 Bacon Road.

CLAPHAM, BARBARA, 28 April 1942. Age 17. 7 Globe Row, Globe Street. Daughter of Ronald Clapham. Died at 7 Globe Row.

CLAPHAM, DAPHNE, 28 April 1942. Age 14. 7 Globe Row, Globe Street. Daughter of Ronald Clapham. Died at 7 Globe Row.

CLARKE, ADA ELIZA, 27 April 1942. Age 70. At 12 Bixfields Buildings, Rupert Street.

CLARKE, JAMES, 30 April 1942. Age 55. Husband of Fernande Louise Aline Clarke, 9 Main Street, Dundrum, Dublin, Irish Republic. Injured 29 April 1942; died at Norwich.

CLAXTON, CECIL, 3 August 1940. Age 56. 7 Victoria Terrace, Horns Lane. Husband of Gertrude Claxton. Injured 30 July 1940, at 7 Victoria Terrace; died at Norfolk and Norwich Hospital.

CLAXTON, GERTRUDE, 30 July 1940. Age 56. 7 Victoria Terrace, Horns Lane. Wife of Cecil Claxton. Died at 7 Victoria Terrace.

CLENDINNING, BLANCHE AGNES, 27 April 1942. Age 51. 44 Southwell Road. Daughter of James and Elizabeth Florence Jolly; widow of Lieutenant Commander Robert Veitch Clendinning, RN. Died at 44 Southwell Road.

CLENDINNING, PAUL VEITCH, Lance Bombardier, 53 Battery, 41 Light Anti-Aircraft Regt, Royal Artillery. Age 20. 44 Southwell Road. Son of Robert Veitch Clendinning and Blanche Agnes Clendinning.

COATES, CHARLES HENRY, 10 June 1945. Age 33. 2 Wright's Yard, Muspole Street. Died at The Lodge, Bowthorpe Road.

CODLING, LILY ELEANOR, 29 April 1942. Age 44. Daughter of Mr S. Smith, 58 Heigham Street; wife of William Codling. Died at 185 Nelson Street.

COPLAND, HARRY CHARLES, 2 August 1942. Age 40. Son of Sidney Charles and Henrietta Copland, 61 Bakers Road; husband of Florence Copland, 120 Drayton Road. Died at Drayton Road.

CORNWELL, MARY ANN, 29 April 1941. Age 67. Widow of A. Cornwell. Died at City Road.

COUZENS, PEGGY MURIEL, 1 August 1940. Age 17. Daughter of W.S. and H.R. Couzens, 4 George Borrow Road. Died at Boulton & Paul's Works.

CRISP, JOHN ARTHUR, 28 April 1942. Aged 4 months. Son of Mr and Mrs Arthur Crisp, 34 Sewell Road. Died at 21 Rye Avenue.

CULYER, FREDERICK, 29 April 1942. Age 56. 14 Livingstone Street. Died at Edinburgh Road.

CURSON, GORDON ARTHUR, 12 May 1942. Age 35. Son of John Roberts Curson, 30 Greyhound Opening. Injured 29 April 1942, at Greyhound Opening, died at the Isolation Hospital.

DANIELS, ROBERT, 10 July 1940. Age 30. Son of the late George and Sarah Daniels; husband of Kathleen Mabel Daniels, 30 Bell Road. Injured 9 July 1940, at Boulton & Paul's Works; died at Norfolk and Norwich Hospital.

DAVISON, JAMES WILLIAM, 27 April 1942. Age 50. ARP Rescue Service. Husband of Ethel Maud Davison, 71 Hotblack Road. Died at Corporation Depot, Westwick Street.

DEBBAGE, WILLIAM GEORGE, 1 August 1940. Age 56. Husband of Ada Florence Debbage, 7 Heigham Grove. Died at Boulton & Paul's Works.

DELAMERE, JOSEPH ROBERT, 27 April 1942. Age 46. Husband of Mary Pauline Delamere Wooddown, The Downs, Mullingar, Co. Westmeath, Irish Republic. Died at 23 Bacon Road.

DIXON, ISOBEL JEAN, 27 April 1942. Age 4. 39 Patteson Road. Daughter of Frank F. Dixon and Laura May Dixon. Died at 39 Patteson Road.

DIXON, LAURA MAY, 27 April 1942. Age 36. 39 Patteson Road. Wife of Frank F. Dixon. Died at 39 Patteson Road.

DOE, CHARLES MONTAGUE, 28 April 1942. Age 63. At The Lodge, Bowthorpe Road.

DORE, ADA, 28 April 1942. Age 72. 140 Essex Street. Wife of John Edward Dore. Died at 140 Essex Street.

DRACASS, GEORGE WILLIAM, 27 April 1942. Age 64. Son of Leslie Dracass, 7 Bakers Road; husband of Emma S. Dracass, 25 Alma Terrace. Died at 182 Waterloo Road.

DYE, HARRY LEONARD, 9 July 1940. Age 35. Husband of Annie Lilian Dye, 28 Berners Street, Aylsham Road. Injured 9 July 1940, at Barnards Ltd; died same day at Norfolk and Norwich Hospital.

EAGLETON, JOSEPH, 28 April 1942. Age 81. 2 Quayside. Died at The Lodge, Bowthorpe Road.

EASTO, LILIAN MAY, 29 April 1942. Age 47. 67 Palgrave Road, Great Yarmouth. Daughter of the late John and Ellen Jane Easto. Died at 75 Earlham Road.

EATHERLEY, EDNA DORIS, 27 April 1942. Age 18. 33 Bacon Road. Daughter of Raymond Lionel and Hilda Ellen Smith; wife of Sergeant Kenneth Eatherley, RAF. Died at 33 Bacon Road.

EDRICH, CATHERINE EVE, 29 April 1942. Age 79. 4 Hill House Road. Daughter of the late George and Sophia Winifred Morris, Prince of Wales Road; widow of Robert Shepherd Edrich. Died at 4 Hill House Road.

ELVIN, FREDERICK 9 July 1940. Age 32. Son of Jack Elvin; husband of Violet May Elvin, 5 Cadge Close, Earlham Estate, Norwich. Died at Barnards Works, Salhouse Road,

EMMS, CHARLES PERCY, 28 April 1942. Age 65. 55 Shipstone Road. Died at The Lodge, Bowthorpe Road.

EVERETT, ETHEL MAUD, 30 July 1940. Age 60. 15 Victoria Terrace, Horns Lane. Daughter of the late Richard Elijah and Ann Everett, 14 Victoria Terrace. Died at 15 Victoria Terrace.

EVERETT, RICHARD CONNELL, 30 July 1940. Age 66. 15 Victoria Terrace, Horns Lane. Son of the late Richard Elijah and Ann Everett, 14 Victoria Terrace; husband of the late Hebe Everett. Died at 15 Victoria Terrace.

FAULKNER, MARY ELLEN, 28 April 1942. Age 61. 19 Rupert Street. Daughter of the late George and Rebecca Tuttle; widow of Ernest Faulkner. Injured at 19 Rupert Street; died same day at Norfolk and Norwich Hospital.

FEEK, DENNIS HERBERT, 1 August 1940. Age 15. Son of Mr and Mrs Herbert Henry Feek, 130 Aylsham Road. Died at Boulton & Paul's Works.

FLOOD, HARRIET, 19 March 1943. Age 50. 99 Pottergate. Died at 99 Pottergate.

FORDER, DOROTHY MAUD, 28 April 1942. Age 34. 60 Elizabeth Fry Road, Earlham Estate. Daughter of Edward Rouse and the late Agnes Rouse, 2 Nursery Terrace, Great Yarmouth; wife of Gunner Walter Charles Forder, R.A. Injured 27 April 1942, at 60 Elizabeth Fry Road; died at Norfolk and Norwich Hospital.

FORDER, JEAN MARY, 28 April 1942. Age 7. 60 Elizabeth Fry Road, Earlham Estate. Daughter of Gunner Walter Charles Forder, RA, and Dorothy Maud Forder. Injured 27 April 1942, at 60 Elizabeth Fry Road; died at Norfolk and Norwich Hospital.

FOX, FLORENCE ELIZABETH, 28 April 1942. Age 45. 73 Belvoir Street. Wife of Reginald Aubrey Fox. Injured at 73 Belvoir Street; died same day at The Lodge, Bowthorpe Road.

FOX, JOYCE KATHLEEN, 28 April 1942. Age 15. 73 Belvoir Street. Daughter of Reginald Aubrey Fox and Florence Elizabeth Fox. Injured at 73 Belvoir Street; died same day at The Lodge, Bowthorpe Road.

FRANKLIN, WILLIAM ROBERT, 28 April 1942. Age 83. 82 Nelson Street. Died at The Lodge, Bowthorpe Road.

FREEMAN, ALICE ELIZABETH, 2 December 1940. Age 59. 47 St John Street. Wife of E.J. Freeman. Died at 47 St John Street.

FREEMAN, CHARLES GEORGE, 9 July 1940. Age 44. Husband of Edith Mary Freeman, 102 Woodcock Road. Died at Thorpe Station Yard.

FREEMAN, LUCRETIA LYDIA, 28 April 1942. Age 72. 25 Rupert Street. Died at 25 Rupert Street.

FULLER, ALBERT EDWARD, 27 April 1942. Age 57. 6 Little Arms Street. Husband of Sarah Agnes Fuller. Died at 6 Little Arms Street.

FULLER, SARAH AGNES, 27 April 1942. Age 60. 6 Little Arms Street. Wife of Albert Edward Fuller. Died at 6 Little Arms Street.

GAFFNEY, LAURENCE, 30 April 1942. Age 47. Courtlough, Balbriggan, Co. Dublin, Irish Republic. Son of the late Laurence and Mary Gaffney. Died at 55 Livingstone Street.

GALEY, JESSIE MARIA, 28 April 1942. Age 70. 25 Rupert Street. Daughter of the late Thomas Edward and Maria Galey, Rutland Street. Died at 25 Rupert Street.

GAMBLE, WINIFRED MAY, 30 April 1942. Age 36. 58 Ella Road. Daughter of William and Jane Hagg, 6 Chalk Hill Road; wife of Private Leonard William Gamble, the Royal Norfolk Regiment. Injured 29 April 1942, at 58 Ella Road; died at Norfolk and Norwich Hospital.

GARNER, FREDERICK, 28 April 1942. Age 50. 25 Esdelle Street. Died at Oak Street.

GAZE, FLORENCE ELIZABETH, 28 April 1942. Age 59. 19 Rupert Street. Wife of William Wesley Gaze. Died at 19 Rupert Street.

GEOGHEGAN, EINRI DAN, 30 April 1942. Age 28. Son of Joseph H. Geoghegan, Ballinsteen, Dundrum, Co. Dublin, Irish Republic. Died at 55 Livingstone Street.

GODDARD, JOAN MIRIAM, 28 April 1942. Age 21. 39 Patterson Road. Wife of Corporal Victor Charles Goddard, RAF. Died at Norfolk and Norwich Hospital.

GOODE, HARRY, 28 April 1942. Age 82, at The Lodge, Bowthorpe Road.

GOREHAM, WALTER, 27 April 1942. Age 46. 43 Patteson Road. Died at 43 Patteson Road.

GRAY, CHARLES EDWARD STAMP, 29 April 1942. Age 36. Son of the late Frederick and Edith Gray; husband of Lilian Gray, 13 Dickens Drive, Laindon, Essex. Died at 49 Buxton Road.

GREAVES, LILY, 1 August 1940. Age 58. 10 Dakin Road. Widow of Robert Greaves. Died at Boulton & Paul's Works.

GREEN, FRANK ROBERT, 28 April 1942. Age 48. Son of Mr and Mrs R. Green, of 87 Eade Road; husband of H.M. Green, 37 Palmer Road. Died at 69 Valpy Avenue.

HAMMOND, HELEN MAIDA, 2 December 1940. Age 50. Daughter of E. and H. Hammond, 98 Spencer Street. Died at 228 King Street.

HANSELL, CHARLOTTE PHOEBE, 28 April 1942. Age 55. 27 Orchard Street. Daughter of Mrs S. Chapman, 71 Knowsley Road; widow of William Russell Hansell. Injured at 27 Orchard Street; died same day at Norfolk and Norwich Hospital.

HARBACH, WILLIAM HENRY, 27 April 1942. Age 47. Home Guard. Son of Joseph and Sarah Ann Harbach, Lilac Lane, Cradley, Worcestershire; husband of Olive Irene Harbach, 17 Elm Grove Lane. Died at Norwich.

HAWES, JESSIE DOUGLAS, 29 April 1942. Age 24. 75 Earlham Road. Daughter of Edwin Jones, 2 James Street, Lincoln, and the late Jessie Douglas Jones; wife of Lance Sergeant Cyril James Hawes, RA. Died at 75 Earlham Road.

HAYHOE, BENJAMIN, 28 April 1942. Age 52. Fire watcher. 7 Clifton Street. Husband of Clara E. Hayhoe. Died at Northumberland Street Shelter.

HEWITT, EMILY MARIA, 27 April 1942. Age 80. 6 Bixfields Buildings, Rupert Street. Widow of John Hewitt. Died at 4 Bixfields Buildings.

HEWITT, LYDIA MAY, 29 April 1942. Age 48. 13 Ethel Road. Wife of Ashley Walter Hewitt. Died at Ethel Road.

HIGH, DAISY MAUD, 18 February 1941. Age 36. 46 Vauxhall Street. Daughter of Ernest E. and Emily S. Horne, 11 Waldeck Road; wife of John Walter High. Died at 46 Vauxhall Street.

HIGH, JOHN WALTER, 18 February 1941. Age 36. St John Ambulance Brigade. 46 Vauxhall Street. Son of John and Christianna High, 27 Bartholomew Street; husband of Daisy Maud High. Died at 46 Vauxhall Street.

HILL, FREDERICK JOSEPH, 28 June 1942. Age 72. Cinder Ovens Row. Died at The Lodge, Bowthorpe Road.

HOLLAND, ANNE, 27 April 1942. Age 78. 45 Patteson Road. Widow of Clement Holland. Died at 45 Patteson Road.

HOLLAND, PATRICK, 27 April 1942. Age 45. St Patrick's, Gorse Avenue, Reepham Road. Son of Anne and of the late Clement Holland. Died at 45 Patteson Road.

HOPWOOD, CHARLES JOSEPH, 2 April 1941. Age 50. Husband of B.M. Hopwood, 32 Spencer Street. Died at Thorpe Station Goods Yard.

HOULT, BERTIE, 9 July 1940. Age 55. Son of Frederick John Hoult, JP, Gresham House, Ethel Road; husband of Kathleen Hoult, 12 Ethel Road. Injured at LNER, Thorpe Station; died same day at Norfolk and Norwich Hospital.

HOUSE, VIOLET MAY, 4 February 1941. Age 34. 91 Plumstead Road. Wife of Jesse Henry House. Died at 91 Plumstead Road.

HOWES, HERBERT ROBERT, 1 August 1940. Age 47. Husband of Elizabeth Frances Howes, 30 Ella Road. Died at Thorpe Station goods yard.

HOWETT, CHARLES, 28 April 1942. Age 76. 24 Bowthorpe Road. Husband of Thirza Howett. Died at 24 Bowthorpe Road.

HOWLETT, GEORGE, 6 May 1941. Age 83. 30 Bury Street. Husband of Emma Maud Howlett. Injured at 30 Bury Street, died same day at Norfolk and Norwich Hospital.

HOWLETT, HANNAH, 2 December 1940. Age 31. 43 St John Street. Wife of F.J. Howlett. Died at 47 St John Street.

HUBBARD, THOMAS, 27 April 1942. Age 52. Home Guard; 35 St Martin's Road. Son of Thomas Hubbard, 175 Sprowston Road; husband of G.M. Hubbard. Died at St Martin's Road.

HUNT, EDITH, 29 April 1942. Age 70. 32 Helena Road. Wife of Ernest Albert Hunt. Died at 32 Helena Road.

HUNT, ELLA, 30 April 1942. Age 59. 52 Winter Road. Daughter of the late Mr and Mrs A.F. Hunt. Died at 52 Winter Road.

HUNT, ERNEST ALBERT, 29 April 1942. Age 67. 32 Helena Road. Husband of Edith Hunt. Died at 32 Helena Road.

JACOB, ALICE, 27 April 1942. Age 78. Daughter of the late Robert and Susanna Jacob of Holt. Died at 73 Adelaide Street.

JARVIS, BERIS MABEL, 27 April 1942. Age 25. 41 Patteson Road. Daughter of Frederick William and May Martha Jarvis. Died at 41 Patteson Road.

JARVIS, DOROTHY EDITH MAY, 27 April 1942. Age 27. 41 Patteson Road. Daughter of Frederick William and May Martha Jarvis. Died at 41 Patteson Road.

JARVIS, FREDERICK WILLIAM, 27 April 1942. Age 60. 41 Patteson Road. Son of Richard and Mary Ann Elizabeth Jarvis, of Briningham; husband of May Martha Jarvis. Died at 41 Patteson Road.

JARVIS, MAY MARTHA, 27 April 1942. Age 56. 41 Patteson Road. Daughter of Mr and Mrs Alfred Lambert of Wickmere; wife of Frederick William Jarvis. Died at 41 Patteson Road.

JEFFRIES, AGNES NOEL, 18 February 1941. Age 26. Wife of H.J. Jeffries. Died at 47 Vauxhall Street.

JOHNSON, AUDREY MAY, 28 April 1942. Age 17. 49 Elm Grove Lane. Daughter of Mr and Mrs Frederic Charles Johnson. Died at 49 Elm Grove Lane.

JOHNSON, DORIS ELSIE MABEL, 30 July 1940. Age 13. 14 Victoria Terrace, Horns Lane. Daughter of George and Mabel Matilda Johnson. Died at 14 Victoria Terrace.

JOHNSON, GEORGE, 30 July 1940. Age 47. 14 Victoria Terrace, Horns Lane. Husband of Mabel Matilda Johnson. Died at 14 Victoria Terrace.

JOHNSON, MABEL MATILDA, 30 July 1940. Age 47. 14 Victoria Terrace, Horns Lane. Wife of George Johnson. Died at 14 Victoria Terrace.

JOLLY, ELIZABETH FLORENCE, 27 April 1942. Age 79. 44 Southwell Road. Daughter of Lawrence and Eliza Neal; wife of James Jolly. Died at 44 Southwell Road.

JOLLY, FLORENCE MAY, 27 April 1942. Age 53. 44 Southwell Road. Daughter of James and Elizabeth Florence Jolly. Died at 44 Southwell Road.

JOLLY, JAMES, 27 April 1942. Age 78. 44 Southwell Road. Son of John and Charlotte Jolly; husband of Elizabeth Florence Jolly. Died at 44 Southwell Road.

JONES, BRIAN MAURICE, 14 January 1945. Age 11. Son of Henry Sidney and Iris Ivy Jones, 16 Marshall Road, Mile Cross Estate. Died at Norwich.

JOPP, ETHEL ADA, 28 April 1942. Age 28. 6 St Mary's Road. Daughter of Charles and Lydia Seaman, 4 Oak Lane, Catton Grove; widow of Sergeant Walter Henry Jopp, RA. Died at 6 St Mary's Road.

KEELEY, ELLEN ELIZABETH, 28 April 1942. Age 64. 132 Millers Lane, St Clement's Hill, New Catton. Wife of Henry Keeley. Died at 132 Millers Lane.

KEELEY, HENRY, 28 April 1942. Age 72. 132 Millers Lane, St Clement's Hill, New Catton. Husband of Ellen Elizabeth Keeley. Died at 132 Millers Lane.

KEMP, ERNEST RICHARD, Fire watcher. Age 61. 6 Cedar Road, Norwich. Husband of the late Madeline Kemp. Injured 27 April 1942 at Lothian Street, Norwich. Died at White Lodge Emergency Hospital, Exning.

KEMP, MARY ELIZABETH, 14 January 1945. Age 5. Daughter of Walter Frederick and Phyllis Kathleen Kemp, 14 Spynke Road, Mile Cross. Died at 14 Spynke Road.

KENT, ROBERT, 27 April 1942. Age 67. Fireman, AFS. Son of the late R. and Emma Maria Kent, Priory Yard, Little Bill Close; husband of Martha Emily Kent, 19 Appleyard Crescent, Mile Cross. Died at Edwards & Holmes Factory, Drayton Road.

KETT, FREDERICK JOHN, 28 April 1942. Age 68. Husband of Alice E. Kett, 117 Ketts Hill. Died at 117 Ketts Hill.

KIDDELL, HERBERT PERCY, 9 July 1940. Age 44. 209 Gertrude Road. Died at Boulton & Paul's Works.

KING, DORIS MAY, 28 April 1942. Age 16. 62 Chapel Field Road. Daughter of Joseph Edward King. Died at Chapel Field Gardens.

KING, HONOR LILIAN, 28 April 1942. Age 14. 62 Chapel Field Road. Daughter of Joseph Edward King. Died at Chapel Field Gardens.

KNIGHTS, BEATRICE, 29 April 1942. Age 62. 35 Alexandra Road. Daughter of the late Frederick and Harriett Knights, 15 Heigham Street. Died at 28 Alexandra Road.

KNIGHTS, JOAN KATHLEEN, 5 September 1942. Age 15. Daughter of Benjamin Rayner and Hilda Knights, 61 Rackham Road. Died at Batson & Webster's Shoe Factory, Fishergate.

LAFFLING, STANLEY DOUGLAS, 9 July 1940. Age 23. Son of Albert and the late Emily Laffling, 3 Gipping Cottages, Bramford, Ipswich, Suffolk; husband of E. May Laffling, 253 Dereham Road. Died at Thorpe Station Engine Sheds.

LAKE, ANN, 27 April 1942. Age 63. 81 Northcote Road. Wife of Thomas Arthur Lake. Died at 81 Northcote Road.

LAKE, THOMAS ARTHUR, 27 April 1942. Age 65. 81 Northcote Road. Husband of Ann Lake. Died at 81 Northcote Road.

LAKEY, THOMAS JOHN, 29 April 1942. Age 25. Son of Thomas William and Myra Ruth Lakey of Whissonsett, East Dereham. Died at 9 Ethel Road.

LAMB, CECIL GEORGE, 27 April 1942. Age 49. Fire watcher. Son of the late Mr T. Lamb; husband of Hilda Lamb, 23 Bowers Avenue. Died at Corporation Depot, Westwick Street.

LEMMON, ALICE MILDRED, 27 April 1942. Age 31. 11 Northumberland Street. Daughter of Mr and Mrs G. Browne, 128 Portland Street; wife of Frederick Charles Lemmon. Died at 11 Northumberland Street.

LEMMON, YVONNE MARION, 27 April 1942. Age 7. 11 Northumberland Street. Daughter of Frederick Charles Lemmon and Alice Mildred Lemmon. Died at 11 Northumberland Street.

LESTER, HETTY SELINA, 27 June 1942. Age 70. At 16 Cotman Road.
LIGGATT, DAVID, 3 August 1941. Patrol Officer, Smethwick AFS. Died at
Norwich.

LINCOLN, JEREMIAH, 28 April 1942. Age 63. Husband of Annie Lincoln,
7 Wiggs Passage, Distillery Street. Died at The Lodge, Bowthorpe Road.

LOCKWOOD, BERYL KATHLEEN, 28 April 1942. Age 11. 65 Rosebery Road.
Daughter of Alfred George Lockwood and Hilda May Lockwood. Died at
65 Rosebery Road.

LOCKWOOD, HILDA MAY, 28 April 1942. Age 37. 65 Rosebery Road. Daughter
of Mrs E. Reeve (formerly Fenn) and the late E. Fenn; wife of Alfred George
Lockwood. Died at 65 Rosebery Road.

LOCKWOOD, JACK REGINALD, 28 April 1942. Age 7. 65 Rosebery Road. Son
of Alfred George Lockwood and Hilda May Lockwood. Died at 65 Rosebery Road.

LOCKWOOD, MARGARET WINIFRED, 28 April 1942. Aged 3 months;
65 Rosebery Road. Daughter of Alfred George Lockwood and Hilda May
Lockwood. Died at 65 Rosebery Road.

LORD, WILLIAM BENJAMIN, 9 July 1940. Age 50. Husband of Harriet Lord,
106 Bowthorpe Road. Injured at LNER, Thorpe Station. Died same day at Norfolk
and Norwich Hospital.

LOVETT, KATE BRADFIELD, 10 July 1940. Age 60. Grange Cottage, Salhouse
Road, Rackheath. Wife of Arthur James Lovett. Injured 9 July 1940, at Grange
Cottage, Salhouse Road. Died at Norfolk and Norwich Hospital.

MACE, RONALD, 19 May 1943. Fireman, NFS. Husband of Lucy Mace,
86 Knowsley Road. Died at Norwich.

McMILLAN, JOHN HENRY, 9 July 1940. Age 60. 235 Littleton Road, Lower
Kersal, Salford, Lancashire. Husband of Miriam McMillan. Injured at Boulton &
Paul's Works; died same day at Norfolk and Norwich Hospital.

MAKIN, ELLEN AGNES, 18 February 1941. Age 27. Wife of Edward Thomas
Makin. Died at 47 Vauxhall Street.

MAKIN, EDWARD THOMAS, 18 February 1941. Age 31. Husband of Ellen
Agnes Makin. Died at 47 Vauxhall Street.

MANN, GEORGE, 27 June 1942. Age 89. Died at 41 Spitalfields.

MEDLER, BARBARA BEATRICE MARY, 1 August 1940. Age 25. Daughter of Bernard Joseph and Beatrice Lucy Gurney, 22 George Borrow Road, Earlham; wife of Stanley C. Medler. Died at Boulton & Paul's Works.

MEEK, WILLIAM HENRY ROBERT, 7 May 1942. Age 82. 11 Midland Street. Died at The Lodge, Bowthorpe Road.

MIDDLETON, LILIAN UNA, 30 April 1942. Age 61. 7 Trafford Road. Daughter of the late Mr and Mrs Thomas Middleton. Died at 7 Trafford Road.

MILLER, JEAN AUDREY, 28 April 1942. Age 8. Daughter of Bertie James Miller, 155 Olney Road, Walworth, London and Maud Helen Miller. Injured 27 April 1942 at 81 Northcote Road; died at Norfolk and Norwich Hospital.

MILLER, MAUD HELEN, 27 April 1942. Age 39. Daughter of Thomas Arthur and Ann Lake; wife of Bertie James Miller, 155 Olney Road, Walworth, London. Died at 81 Northcote Road.

MILLER, SHEILA ANN, 27 April 1942. Age 5. Daughter of Bertie James Miller, 155 Olney Road, Walworth, London and Maud Helen Miller. Died at 81 Northcote Road.

MINISTER, FLORENCE HANNAH, 2 May 1942. Age 44. 15 Northumberland Street. Wife of Stoker Edmund George Minister, RN. Injured 27 April 1942 at 15 Northumberland Street; died at Norfolk and Norwich Hospital.

MINISTER, VALERIE, 27 April 1942. Age 3. 15 Northumberland Street. Daughter of Stoker Edmund George Minister, RN, and Florence Hannah Minister. Died at 15 Northumberland Street.

MINTER, MAY BEATRICE, 28 April 1942. Age 48. 117 Philadelphia Lane. Wife of Christopher Minter. Died at 113 Philadelphia Lane.

MONAGHAN, SARAH, 27 April 1942. Age 52. 45 Patteson Road. Daughter of Anne and the late Clement Holland; wife of John Monaghan. Died at 45 Patteson Road.

MOORE, LILY AGNES, 28 April 1942. Age 47. 55 Union Street. Wife of Bertie James Moore. Died at Norfolk and Norwich Hospital.

MOORE, SABINA ELIZABETH, 29 April 1942. Age 60. 46 Alexandra Road. Widow of Herbert Sidney Moore. Died at 46 Alexandra Road.

MUIRHEAD, NEVILLE RICHARD GORDON, 27 June 1942. Age 18. Son of J. Walter and Laura Muirhead, of Barjuli, Assam, India. Died at 36 Bracondale.

NASH, AUDREY ELEANOR, 27 April 1942. Age 49. 52 Southwell Road. Daughter of Eleanor Seely and the late Herbert Thomas Seely; wife of Arthur James Nash. Died at 52 Southwell Road.

NASH, ARTHUR JAMES, 27 April 1942. Age 41. 52 Southwell Road. Son of Charlotte Nash; husband of Audrey Eleanor Nash. Died at 52 Southwell Road.

NEVE, AGNES JULIA, 29 April 1942. Age 85. Widow of William Neve. Died at 29 Alexandra Road.

NEWBY, BARBARA OLIVE, 27 April 1942. Age 8. Walnut Tree Shades, Old Post Office, Castle Street. Daughter of Walter Newby and Hilda Newby. Died at 54 Patteson Road.

NEWBY, HILDA, 27 April 1942. Age 45. Walnut Tree Shades, Old Post Office, Castle Street. Daughter of E.H. and Kate John, 45 St Barnabas Court, Midland Street; wife of Walter Newby. Died at 54 Patteson Road.

NEWMAN, LEAH ALICE, 30 July 1940. Age 56. 5 Victoria Terrace, Horns Lane. Daughter of William and Sarah Hardy, Coslany Street; wife of Robert Henry Newman. Died at 5 Victoria Terrace.

NEWMAN, ROBERT HENRY, 30 July 1940. Age 58. 5 Victoria Terrace, Horns Lane. Son of Charles and Harriet Newman, Waterloo Road; husband of Leah Alice Newman. Died at 5 Victoria Terrace.

NEWRUCK, Elizabeth Ann, 2 May 1942. Age 71. 47 Aylsham Road, Norwich. Daughter of the late Thomas George Newruck. Injured at Norwich. Died same day at White Lodge Emergency Hospital, Exning.

NINHAM, MARTHA, 27 April 1942. Age 73. 2 William Street. Widow of Frederic Ninham. Died at 2 William Street.

O'TOOLE, JOHN, 27 April 1942. Age 25. Son of Elizabeth O'Toole, 13 Convent Road, Wicklow, Irish Republic. Died at 23 Bacon Road.

PAGE, ANNE, 28 April 1942. Age 81. 6 Globe Row, Globe Street. Widow of William Walter Page. Died at 6 Globe Row.

PALMER, CECIL CHARLES HENRY, 27 April 1942. Age 45. Fire watcher. 12 Clarke Road. Son of Emily Palmer, 246 Silver Road, and the late Charles Henry Palmer; husband of the late Ethel Bessie Palmer. Died at Edwards & Holmes' Factory, Drayton Road.

PALMER, ERNEST WILLIAM, 27 April 1942. Age 65. 48 Southwell Road. Husband of Mary Ann Palmer. Died at 48 Southwell Road.

PALMER, MARY ANN, 27 April 1942. Age 65. 48 Southwell Road. Wife of
Ernest William Palmer. Died at 48 Southwell Road.

PARKE, ANNIE BLANCHE, 27 April 1942. Age 77. Wife of George Robert
Parke. Died at 42 Southwell Road.

PARKE, GEORGE ROBERT, 27 April 1942. Age 71. Husband of Annie Blanche
Parke. Died at 42 Southwell Road.

PARKE, HILDA LOUISA, 27 April 1942. Age 37. Daughter of George Robert and
Annie Blanche Parke. Died at 42 Southwell Road.

PARKER, HAROLD GEORGE ROWING, 1 August 1940. Age 32. Glencoe,
Marlborough Road, Oulton Broad, Lowestoft, Suffolk. Son of Mr and Mrs George
Edgar Rowing Parker. Died at Boulton & Paul's Works.

PARKER, RICHARD ALBERT, 9 July 1940. Age 37. Son of Mr W. Parker,
8 Belsize Road; husband of Ivy M. Parker, 5 Samuel Road. Injured at Thorpe
Station engine sheds. Died same day at Norfolk and Norwich Hospital.

PAYNE, GEORGE ARTHUR, 9 July 1940. Age 37. Husband of R. Payne, 79 Bull
Close Road. Died at Thorpe Station engine sheds.

PEARCE, JAMES, 28 April 1942. Age 53. Husband of Dora Angelina Pearce,
24 Jubilee Avenue, East Dereham. Died at 22 Northumberland Street.

PEARCE, RUSSELL LEONARD, 25 March 1942. Fireman, NFS. Husband of
B.M. Pearce, 17 Newton Street, Ipswich, Suffolk. Died at Norwich.

PEDERSON, ANDERS HAAGEN, 29 April 1942. Age 56. Danish Subject,
11 Brancaster Lane, Purley, Surrey. Husband of Dagmar Pederson. Died at
Hippodrome, St Giles Street.

PEDERSON, DAGMAR, 29 April 1942. Age 53. Danish Subject, 11 Brancaster
Lane, Purley, Surrey. Daughter of Mrs Sanger, of Burstow Lodge, Purley, Surrey, and
the late John Sanger; wife of Anders Haagen Pederson. Died at Hippodrome,
St Giles Street.

PENNYMORE, ARTHUR JOHN, 2 December 1940. Age 55. 70 Bracondale.
Died at Bracondale.

PITCHFORD, GERTRUDE IRENE, 29 April 1942. Age 27. Wife of Harold
Leslie Pitchford. Killed in a caravan at the Hippodrome, St Giles Street.

PITCHFORD, HAROLD LESLIE, 29 April 1942. Age 44. Husband of Gertrude
Irene Pitchford. Resident stage manager, killed in a caravan at the Hippodrome
Theatre, St Giles Street.

PLAYFORD, BERTHA ROSE, 9 July 1940. Age 19. Daughter of Mrs R.H. Playford, 27 Copeman Street, Pottergate, and the late J. Playford. Injured at Carrow Hill; died same day at Norfolk and Norwich Hospital.

PLUMMER, REBECCA, 27 April 1942. Age 65. 7 Bixfields Buildings, Rupert Street. Died at 7 Bixfields Buildings.

POSTLE, EMILY, 29 April 1942. Age 90. Unthank Road. Daughter of the late George and Sophia Winifred Morris; widow of William Postle. Died at 4 Hill House Road.

POTTER, BRIAN ROYAL, 28 April 1942. Age 10. 6 St Mary's Road. Son of Aircraftman Second Class Royal Potter, RAF, and Lilian Potter. Died at 6 St Mary's Road.

POTTER, LILIAN, 28 April 1942. Age 30. 6 St Mary's Road. Daughter of Charles and Lydia Seaman, 4 Oak Lane, Catton Grove; wife of Aircraftman Second Class Royal Potter, RAF. Died at 6 St Mary's Road.

POTTER, NOVA, 28 April 1942. Age 3. 6 St Mary's Road. Daughter of Aircraftman Second Class Royal Potter, RAF, and Lilian Potter. Died at 6 St Mary's Road.

POTTER, ROYAL, Aircraftman Second Class, 150 Squadron, Royal Air Force Volunteer Reserve. 28 April 1942. Age 27. Son of Clifford and Rosa Potter of Mile Cross, husband of Lilian Potter and father of Brian and Nova Potter, all of whom were killed in the same incident at 6 St Mary's Road.

PREST, EVELYN BESSIE, 28 April 1942. Age 45. 59 Nelson Street, Dereham Road. Daughter of Martha and of the late Edward Prest. Injured at 59 Nelson Street; died same day at Norfolk and Norwich Hospital.

PREST, MARTHA, 28 April 1942. Age 76. 59 Nelson Street. Widow of Edward Prest. Injured at 59 Nelson Street, died same day at Norfolk and Norwich Hospital.

RABY, ELLEN, 1 August 1940. Age 63. Wife of S. Raby, 114 Shorncliffe Avenue, Drayton Road. Died at Boulton & Paul's Works.

RABY, WILLIAM, 1 May 1942. Age 73. Husband of Rosina Rebecca Raby, of Goldwell Road, Hall Road. Injured 27 April 1942, at 97 Goldwell Road; died at Norfolk and Norwich Hospital.

RAVEN, CYRIL ROBERT, 28 April 1942. Age 41. Son of Mr R.G. Raven, 27 Quebec Road. Died at 49 St Leonard's Road.

RAVEN, GLADYS PATRICIA, 28 April 1942. Age 17. Daughter of Cyril Robert Raven. Died at 49 St Leonard's Road.

RAVEN, ZENA MARY, 28 April 1942. Age 15. Daughter of Cyril Robert Raven. Died at 49 St Leonard's Road.

READ, ALFRED ERNEST, 27 April 1942. Age 39. Husband of Winifred Read. Died at 87 The Avenue.

READ, ALBERT SAMUEL, 6 February 1943. Age 35. Fireman, NFS. Husband of Evelyn Alice Read, 103 Bury Street, Unthank Road. Died at Lads' Club.

READ, CLIFFORD ROBERT, 28 June 1942. Age 77. 55 Hall Road. Son of Ransom and Louisa Read, 16 Hereford Street, Bethnal Green, London. Injured 27 June 1942, at 55 Hall Road; died at The Lodge, Bowthorpe Road.

RISEBOROUGH, WILLIAM GREEN, 27 April 1942. Age 65. 362 Dereham Road. Husband of Mary Ann Riseborough. Died at 362 Dereham Road.

RIX, JAMES, 28 April 1942. Age 67. 29 Rose Yard. Died at The Lodge, Bowthorpe Road.

ROBINSON, FLORENCE MAY, 30 April 1942. Age 19. Daughter of Minnie Emily Robinson, 218 Heigham Street, and Samuel John Robinson. Died at Heigham Street.

ROBINSON, SAMUEL JOHN, 30 April 1942. Age 52. Husband of Minnie Emily Robinson, 218 Heigham Street. Injured at Heigham Street; died same day at The Lodge, Bowthorpe Road.

RUDRAM, FREDERICK ALBERT, 5 September 1942. Age 27. Son of Albert Mark and Ellen Rudram, 40 Muriel Road; husband of Ruby Violet Rudram, 2 Boundary Avenue, Mile Cross. Died at Frazer's Joinery Works.

SAMPSON, GLADYS ROSE, 10 July 1940. Age 18. 29 Gloucester Street. Daughter of Mr E.J. Sampson. Injured 9 July 1940, at Carrow Hill; died at Norfolk and Norwich Hospital.

SANDELL, ARTHUR ROBERT, 29 April 1941. Age 48. Husband of Grace Frances Sandell, 244 King Street. Died at Oat Mills, Carrow Works.

SAUNDERS, MURIEL LOUISA ELIZABETH, 27 April 1942. Age 24. 10 Stafford Street. Wife of Corporal Leslie P.W. Saunders, RAF. Died at 10 Helena Road.

SAVORY, FLORENCE MAY, 29 April 1942. Age 16. Daughter of Leading Aircraftman A.W. Savory, RAF, and G.M. Savory, 9 Shorncliffe Avenue, Junction Road. Died at 26 Dakin Road.

SAYER, ALBERT ERNEST, 9 July 1940 Age 53. 35 St Peter's Street, Norwich. Died at Barnards Works, Salhouse Road, Sprowston.

SCOTT, EMILY CONSTANCE, 28 April 1942. Age 54. Widow of John Scott. Died at 45 Elm Grove Lane.

SCOTT, THOMAS, 27 June 1942. Age 50. Husband of F.A. Scott. Died at 6 Vincent Road.

SEAGER, ARTHUR GEORGE, 18 February 1941. Age 73. 41 Walpole Street, Vauxhall Street. Died at 41 Walpole Street.

SEAGER, RICHARD LEECH, 18 February 1941. Age 15. 41 Walpole Street, Vauxhall Street. Son of Gladys Maud Smith. Died at 41 Walpole Street.

SELF, WILLIAM, 27 April 1942. Age 51. Fire watcher. Husband of Ethel Amelia Self, 86 Philadelphia Lane. Died at Edwards & Holmes' Factory, Drayton Road.

SEWELL, JAMES FREDERICK, 27 April 1942. Age 48. ARP fire watcher. Son of the late James and Agnes Sewell, New Street, Holt; husband of Florence Edith Sewell, 27 Harlington Avenue, Reepham Road. Died at Corporation Depot, Westwick Street.

SEWTER, CARLOS ANTHONY, 12 July 1940. Age 46. Son of the late Edward and Amelia Sewter, Mill Farm, Lyng; husband of Rose Sewter, Little Melton. Injured 9 July 1940, at Boulton & Paul's Works; died at Norfolk and Norwich Hospital.

SHELDON, SARAH ANNE, 29 April 1942. Age 72. Wife of Alfred Ernest Sheldon, 202 Nelson Street, Dereham Road. Died at 202 Nelson Street.

SHREEVE, Arthur Leonard, 9 July 1940. Age 30. Home Guard. Son of Alice M. Shreeve, of 53 Wymer Street, Norwich, and the late John Spanton Shreeve. Died at Barnards Works, Salhouse Road.

SHRIMPLIN, BENJAMIN, 27 June 1942. Age 75. 39 Spitalfields. Died at Norfolk and Norwich Hospital.

SILOM, ERNEST ROBERT, 9 July 1940. Age 58. Husband of Alice Silom, 41 North Walsham Road, Old Catton. Died at Thorpe Station yard.

SKINNER, HANNAH ELIZABETH, 28 April 1942. Age 70. 33 Albany Road. Daughter of the late Joseph and Betsy Emery, of Chatteris, Cambridgeshire; widow of Abraham Skinner. Died at 33 Albany Road.

SMITH, ALBERT EDWARD HEYHOE, 28 April 1942. Age 51. 1 Rye Avenue. Died at Norwich.

SMITH, ALBERT GEORGE, 30 April 1942. Age 50. Air Raid Warden. Son of W. and R. Smith, 34 Wymer Street, Heigham Road; husband of Kathleen Smith, 56 Alexandra Road. Injured 29 April 1942, at 56 Alexandra Road; died at The Lodge, Bowthorpe Road.

SMITH, ALICE KATE, 27 April 1942. Age 68. 23 Helena Road. Daughter of the late Robert George and Ellen Maria Hill; wife of Alfred Smith. Died at 33 Bacon Road.

SMITH, EDITH MAY, 27 June 1942. Age 30. 4 Vincent Road. Daughter of Mr and Mrs Percy Goreham, 99 Portland Street; wife of Harry George Smith. Died at 6 Vincent Road.

SMITH, EMILY MARY, 29 April 1942. Age 51. Daughter of William Burnham, 201 Nelson Street, and the late Sarah Burnham; wife of Albert Mark Smith, 14 Raynham Street. Died at Raynham Street Shelter.

SMITH, GEORGE GAMMON, 5 September 1942. Age 43. Special Constable. Son of Frederick and Mary Jane Smith, 10 Charles Street; husband of May Elsie Smith, 75 Patteson Road. Died at Batson & Webster's Factory, Fishergate.

SMITH, GRAHAM GOREHAM, 27 June 1942. Age 6 months. 4 Vincent Road. Son of Harry George and Edith May Smith. Died at 6 Vincent Road.

SMITH, HARRY GEORGE, 27 June 1942. Age 34. 4 Vincent Road. Son of E.R. Smith, 4 Belsize Road, and the late Ben Smith; husband of Edith May Smith. Died at 6 Vincent Road.

SMITH, HERBERT RICHARD, 6 May 1941. Age 55. 28 Bury Street. Son of Mrs Smith, 28 Sunny Hills, Lakenham; husband of Maud Agnes Smith. Injured at 28 Bury Street; died same day at Norfolk and Norwich Hospital.

SMITH, HILDA ELLEN, 27 April 1942. Age 43. Fire watcher. 33 Bacon Road. Daughter of Alfred Smith and Alice Kate Smith; wife of Raymond Lionel Smith. Died at 33 Bacon Road.

SMITH, HORACE, 27 April 1942. Age 41. Air Raid Warden. Son of William and Martha Smith, 8 Winchcombe Road, Newbury, Berkshire; husband of Florence Mary Smith, 3 Fairstead Road, Sprowston. Near Gate House, Dereham Road.

SMITH, MALCOLM GOREHAM, 27 June 1942. Age 5. 4 Vincent Road. Son of Harry George and Edith May Smith. Died at 6 Vincent Road.

SMITH, MAUD AGNES, 6 May 1941. Age 51. 28 Bury Street. Daughter of Mr and Mrs Smith, Carrow Road; wife of Herbert Richard Smith. Injured at 28 Bury Street; died same day at Norfolk and Norwich Hospital.

SMITH, RAYMOND LIONEL, 27 April 1942. Age 53. Fire watcher. 33 Bacon Road. Son of Mrs B.E. Smith, 36 Grosvenor Road; husband of Hilda Ellen Smith. Died at 33 Bacon Road.

SMITH, WALTER GEORGE, 9 July 1940. Age 23. Son of W.J. and F.E. Smith, 114 Vincent Road. Died at Boulton & Paul's Works.

SPINKS, BETTY ALEXANDRA, 27 April 1942. Age 25. 48 Southwell Road. Daughter of Ernest William and Mary Ann Palmer; wife of Harry Samuel Spinks. Died at 48 Southwell Road.

SPINKS, CATHERINE MARY, 27 April 1942. Aged 13 months; 48 Southwell Road. Daughter of Harry Samuel Spinks and Betty Alexandra Spinks. Died at 48 Southwell Road.

SPRUCE, LILIAN MABEL, 9 May 1942. Age 32. Octagon Farm, Bixley. Daughter of Mrs F. Hewitt, Mill Haven, Woodton, Bungay, Suffolk; wife of Hubert Marston Spruce. Died at The Lodge, Bowthorpe Road.

SQUIRE, MARY, 2 August 1942. Aged 1 week. Daughter of Bombardier Frank Squire, RA, and Edith Florence Squire, 6 Walpole Road, Great Yarmouth. Died at Sunnyside Nursing Home, Drayton Road.

STANNARD, NELLIE ELIZABETH, 1 May 1942. Age 60. 21 Rowington Road. Wife of Donald Henry Stannard. Injured 30 April 1942 at 21 Rowington Road; died at Norfolk and Norwich Hospital.

STARLING, ELIZA, 7 May 1942. Age 62. 20 Traverse Street. Wife of Sidney John Starling. Injured 27 April 1942, at 20 Traverse Street; died at The Lodge, Bowthorpe Road.

STARLING, HILDA, 28 April 1942. Age 41. 20 Traverse Street. Daughter of Sidney John Starling and Eliza Starling. Injured 27 April 1942, at 20 Traverse Street; died at The Lodge, Bowthorpe Road.

STEVENS, ROY, 29 April 1942. Age 20. Air Raid Warden. Son of Mr F.F. Stevens, 12 Parr Road. Died at Mile Cross Road.

STRIKE, ARTHUR SAMUEL, 9 July 1940. Age 23. Son of Elizabeth Rant (formerly Strike), 23 Clarkson Road. Died at Boulton & Paul's Works.

STROWGER, GEORGE, 9 July 1940. Age 27. Husband of May Eleanor Strowger, 33 Horning Close, North Earlham. Died at Boulton & Paul's Works.

SULLIVAN, JOHN, 29 July 1942. Age 65. 100 Wolseley Road, Great Yarmouth, Norfolk. Injured at Norwich in May 1942. Died at White Lodge Emergency Hospital, Exning.

THAYNE, MARIA, 16 May 1942. Age 82. 8 Globe Row, Globe Street, South Heigham. Widow of William Thayne. Injured at 8 Globe Row; died same day at White Lodge Emergency Hospital, Exning.

TIDD, NOAH, 30 April 1942. Age 53. Husband of L.M. Tidd, 10 Bath House Yard, Oak Street. Died at Old Palace Road.

TIMPSON, MARY ANN, 18 February 1941. Age 70. At 49 Vauxhall Street.

TOOLE, STEPHEN, 5 September 1942. Age 39. Fireman, NFS. Son of Margaret Toole, 187 Gertrude Road, Sprowston Road; husband of Elizabeth S. Toole, 92 Plumstead Road East, Thorpe. Died at Frazer's Joinery Works.

TURNER, ARTHUR, 28 April 1942. Age 41. 1 Read's Buildings, Globe Street. Son of William and Harriett Turner, 151 Essex Street; husband of Edith Blanche Turner. Died at 1 Read's Buildings.

TURNER, CLARA MAY, 28 April 1942. Age 51. 3 Globe Row, Globe Street. Wife of Frederick Thomas Turner. Died at 3 Globe Row.

TURNER, FREDERICK THOMAS, 28 April 1942. Age 54. 3 Globe Row, Globe Street. Husband of Clara May Turner. Died at 3 Globe Row.

TUTTLE, ALICE REBECCA, 28 April 1942. Age 70. 19 Rupert Street. Daughter of the late George and Rebecca Tuttle. Died at 19 Rupert Street.

UPTON, BESSIE GLADYS, 9 July 1940. Age 36. Daughter of Mrs E.H. Upton, 40 Lewis Street, Lakenham, and the late S. Upton. Died at Carrow Hill.

URQUHART, JOHN MACINTOSH, 28 April 1942. Age 73. 90 Rosebery Road. Died at The Lodge, Bowthorpe Road.

UTTING, BERTRAM EDWARD, 29 April 1942. Age 41. 39 Midland Street. Son of Brian E. Utting, West Farm, Attleborough; husband of Beatrice Utting. Died at Greyhound Opening.

VINCENT, GERTRUDE, 28 April 1942. Age 53. Wife of A.J. Vincent, Avenue House, Wroxham. Died at 72 Millers Lane.

WALKER, HENRY PLANE, 28 April 1942. Age 64. Son of John H.P. Walker, 129 Spencer Street; husband of Annie Elizabeth Plane Walker, of the same address. Died at 129 Spencer Street.

WALLACE, ALBERT EDWARD ARTHUR HENRY, 27 April 1942. Age 65. 10 Helena Road. Husband of Louisa Wallace. Died at 10 Helena Road.

WALLACE, ARTHUR, 27 April 1942. Age 29. 10 Helena Road. Son of Albert Edward Arthur Henry and Louisa Wallace. Died at 10 Helena Road.

WALLACE, LOUISA, 27 April 1942. Age 50. 10 Helena Road. Wife of Albert Edward Arthur Henry Wallace. Died at 10 Helena Road.

WALLER, ARTHUR PEACH, 4 February 1941. Age 75. 93 Plumstead Road. Husband of R. Waller. Died at 93 Plumstead Road.

WARD, CONSTANCE MABEL, 28 April 1942. Age 42. 69 Valpy Avenue. Daughter of Mabel Adams, 5 Ashford Street; widow of Robert Ward. Died at 69 Valpy Avenue.

WARD, JOAN EVELYN, 28 April 1942. Age 10. 69 Valpy Avenue. Daughter of Constance Mabel and the late Robert Ward. Died at 69 Valpy Avenue.

WARD, OLIVE MAY, 28 April 1942. Age 20. 69 Valpy Avenue. Daughter of Constance Mabel and the late Robert Ward. Died at 69 Valpy Avenue.

WARD, RICHARD, 28 April 1942. Age 18. 69 Valpy Avenue. Son of Constance Mabel and the late Robert Ward. Died at 69 Valpy Avenue.

WARNES, EILEEN GERTRUDE, 11 December 1940. Age 18. Daughter of John Henry and Kate Eliza Warnes, 258 King Street. Died at 10 The Vale, Carrow Hill.

WARREN, FREDERICK THOMAS, Private, Royal Army Ordnance Corps. 28 April 1942. Age 33. Son of Arthur George and Eliza Warren; husband of Norah Marion Warren of Harringay.

WATERS, AGNES ELIZABETH, 30 April 1942. Age 54. 78 Helena Road. Wife of Albert Edmund Waters. Died at 76 Helena Road.

WATERS, BRENDA LAVINIA, 30 April 1942. Age 17. 78 Helena Road. Daughter of Albert Edmund Waters and Agnes Elizabeth Waters. Died at 76 Helena Road.

WATERS, EDWARD ALAN, 30 April 1942. Age 15. 78 Helena Road. Son of Albert Edmund Waters and Agnes Elizabeth Waters. Died at 76 Helena Road.

WATERS, SYBIL HILDA, 30 April 1942. Age 19. ARP ambulance attendant; 78 Helena Road. Daughter of Albert Edmund Waters and Agnes Elizabeth Waters. Died at 76 Helena Road.

WATSON, REGINALD LESLIE, 5 September 1942. Age 28. Home Guard. Husband of Dora Eleanor Watson, 163 Sprowston Road. Died at Frazer's Joinery Works.

WEBB, GERTRUDE ELIZABETH, 27 April 1942. Age 62. 5 Bixfields Buildings, Rupert Street. Daughter of the late Joshua Webb. Died at 5 Bixfields Buildings.

WELLS, MAY REDGRAVE, 29 April 1942. Age 66. Died at 5A Earlham Road.

WHALL, GEORGE, 28 April 1942. Age 56. 67 Rosebery Road. Husband of Gertrude Whall. Died at 67 Rosebery Road.

WHALL, GERTRUDE, 28 April 1942. Age 54. 67 Rosebery Road. Wife of George Whall. Died at 67 Rosebery Road.

WHITE, BESSIE LOUISA, 27 April 1942. Age 38. 10 Little Arms Street. Daughter of the late Mr and Mrs H.G. Thrower; wife of Donald Wilfred White. Died at 10 Little Arms Street.

WHITE, DONALD WILFRED, 27 April 1942. Age 38. 10 Little Arms Street. Son of Mrs A.W. White, 78 College Road, and the late W. White; husband of Bessie Louisa White. Died at 10 Little Arms Street.

WILBY, ARTHUR, 27 June 1942. Age 3. Constable, Police War Reserve; 55 Junction Road. Son of Elizabeth Wilby, 44 Magdalen Close, and the late Charles Wilby; husband of Kate Maud Wilby. Injured at St Mark's Church; died same day at Norfolk and Norwich Hospital.

WILBY, KATE, 28 April 1942. Age 69. 88 Nicholas Street. Daughter of the late Henry Wilby. Injured at 88 Nicholas Street; died same day at Norfolk and Norwich Hospital.

WILLIAMSON, EMMA, 29 April 1942. Age 73. 11 Bixfields Buildings, Rupert Street. Widow of George Williamson. Injured 27 April 1942, at 11 Bixfields Buildings; died at Norfolk and Norwich Hospital.

WITHERICK, EMMA SARAH ANN, 28 April 1942. Age 74. Widow of Frank Witherick. Died at 18 Rose Valley.

WOOD, ALICE ELVINA, 28 April 1942. Age 56. 146 Drayton Road. Wife of Arthur Frederick Wood. Injured 27 April 1942, at 146 Drayton Road; died at Wardens' Post, Drayton Road.

WOODROW, LEONARD CHARLES, 28 April 1942. Age 34. Son of William and Sarah Woodrow, 75 Leicester Street; husband of Kathleen Woodrow, 43 Junction Road. Died in ambulance at Oak Street.

WRIGHT, FREDERICK, 9 July 1940. Age 16. Son of Mrs E. Wright, 21 Hunter Road. Died at Boulton & Paul's Works.

WRIGHT, HELEN, 29 April 1942. Age 78. 1 Ella Road, Thorpe Hamlet. Widow of Robert William Wright. Died at 1 Ella Road.

WRIGHT, REGINALD EDWARD, 27 April 1942. Age 11. 11 Little Arms Street. Son of Aircraftman First Class Reginald William Wright, RAF. Died at 6 Little Arms Street.

YALLOP, ERNEST EDWARD, 28 April 1942. Age 64. 5 Quayside. Died at The Lodge, Bowthorpe Road.

YALLOP, JAMES, 28 April 1942. Age 69. 125 Ber Street. Died at The Lodge, Bowthorpe Road.

SELECT BIBLIOGRAPHY

Banger, Joan, *Norwich at War* (Albion, 1982).

Bowyer, Michael J.F., *Air Raid! The Enemy Offensive Against East Anglia* (Patrick Stephens, 1986).

Brown, R. Douglas, *East Anglia 1939* (Dalton, 1980).

Brown, R. Douglas, *East Anglia 1940* (Dalton, 1981).

Brown, R. Douglas, *East Anglia 1941* (Dalton, 1986).

Brown, R. Douglas, *East Anglia 1942* (Dalton, 1988).

Brown, R. Douglas, *East Anglia 1943* (Dalton, 1990).

Brown, R. Douglas, *East Anglia 1944* (Dalton, 1992).

Brown, R. Douglas, *East Anglia 1945* (Dalton, 1994).

Collier, Basil, *The Battle of the V-Weapons 1944–45* (Elmfield, 1964).

Collis, Bob, *The Story of the 1942 German Baedeker Raids Against East Anglia* (Flixton, 1993).

Cooper, A.P., *The Changing Face of Norwich* (Cooper, 1948).

Fairhead, Huby, *Decoy Sites: Wartime Deception in Norfolk and Suffolk* (Monograph, 1996).

Freeman, Roger A., *Airfields of the Eighth: Then and Now* (After the Battle, 2001).

Freeman, Roger A., *The Mighty Eighth* (Arms & Armour, 1989).

Hoare, Adrian, *Standing Up to Hitler* (Reeve 1997).

Kemp, Lt Commander P.K., RN, *History of the Royal Norfolk Regiment 1919–1951* (Regimental Association, 1953).

Kent, Arnold, and Andrew Stephenson, *Norwich Inheritance* (Jarrold, 1948).

Le Grice, Edward Charles, *Norwich, The Ordeal of 1942* (Soman Wherry, 1945).

Meeres, Frank, *Norfolk in the Second World War* (Phillimore, 2006).

Morson, Maurice, *A Force Remembered* (Breedon, 2000).

Mottram, R.H., *Assault Upon Norwich* (Soman Wherry, 1945).

Osborne, Mike, *20th Century Defences in Britain: Norfolk* (Concrete, 2008).

Ramsey, Winston G. (ed.), *The Blitz Then and Now September 1939–September 1940* (After the Battle, 1987).

Ramsey, Winston G. (ed.), *The Blitz Then and Now September 1940–May 1941* (After the Battle, 1988).

Ramsey, Winston G. (ed.), *The Blitz Then and Now May 1941–May 1945* (After the Battle, 1987).

Storey, Neil, *Norfolk in the Second World War* (Halsgrove, 2010).

Storey, Neil, *The Pride of Norfolk* (Halsgrove, 2009).

Swain, George, *Norwich Under Fire* (Jarrold, 1945).

Temple, Clifford, *Norwich* (Panda, 1983).

Tillett, Iris, *The Cinderella Army* (Tillett, 1988).

Veriod, Brian S., *A History of the Norwich City Fire Brigade* (Veriod, 1986).

Whiting, Charles, *Three Star Blitz: Baedeker Raids and the Start of Total War, 1942–45* (Leo Cooper, 1987).

Wood, Derek, *Attack Warning Red: Royal Observer Corps and the Defence of Britain 1925 to 1992* (Carmichael & Sweet, 1992).

NEWSPAPERS & MAGAZINES

The Times, The Daily Mail, The Daily Mirror, Norwich Wardens Post, Eastern Daily Press, Eastern Evening News, Norfolk Chronicle, Diss Express, Yarmouth Mercury, East Anglian Daily Times, The Britannia: Regimental Journal of the Royal Norfolk Regiment, The Carrow Works Magazine.

WEBSITES:

BBC People's War: www.bbc.co.uk/history/ww2peopleswar

Commonwealth War Graves Commission: cwgc.org

The Defence of Britain Archive: archaeologydataservice.ac.uk/archives/view/dob/

Historic England: pastscape.org.uk

ACKNOWLEDGEMENTS

I would like to record my gratitude to all those who have contributed to and encouraged my research over the years. Some of those named have sadly passed away but the memories, stories and photographs they shared live on. I would particularly like to thank:

Norfolk Heritage Centre, Norfolk Record Office, Imperial War Museum, National Archives, Commonwealth War Graves Commission, 2nd Air Division Memorial Library, Royal Norfolk Regimental Museum, BBC Radio Norfolk, Anglia Television, Norwich Society, Norfolk Constabulary Archives (John Mason and Peter Pilgram), Norfolk Fire Service (Bruce Hogg and Brian Veriod), Norfolk Family History Society, Judy Ball, Joan Banger, Clifford Temple, Ray Cossey, Frank Kett, Reg Ford, Andy Anderson, Norman Wiltshire, Colonel John Boag, Lieutenant Colonel Alan Cubitt, Major Tom Hall, Major Tom Eaton, Major Monty Smyth, Major Gary Walker, George Clapham, Fred Eva, Fred Howell, Arthur Hewitt, Harry Barnard, John Slaughter, Olive Small, Henry Hansell, Pip Miller, Pru Page, Roy Scott, Barbara Walker, Peter Brooks, Colin Tooke, Norman Bacon, Bob Collis, Richard Cynan-Jones, Keith and Susan Panton. Last but by no means least, I would like to express my heartfelt thanks to my partner Fiona and my loving family.

INDEX